WE ARE ALL COLUMBINE

According to the Distaster Center: In 1999, more than 15,522 people were the victims of homicide in the United States.

Thirteen of those murders occurred at Columbine High School.

Stop violence before it begins.

Violence prevention:
https://www.cdc.gov/violenceprevention/about/index.html

Suicide prevention:
https://www.cdc.gov/suicide/index.html

Mental health assistance:
https://www.samhsa.gov/find-help

A Columbine Book:

WE ARE ALL COLUMBINE

25 Years of Healing

C. SHEPARD

OVERVIEW PUBLISHING

This publication is designed to provide accurate and authoritative information regarding the subject matter covered. While all efforts have been made to ensure accuracy and contact individuals involved, the publisher and author make no guarantees with respect to the accuracy or completeness of the contents of this book and assume no liabilities for errors.

Copyright © 2024 C Shepard.

All rights reserved.

All rights reserved.

No part of this publication may be reproduced, distributed, or transmitted in any form or by any means, electronic or mechanical, including photocopying, recording, or by any information storage or retrieval system without the written permission of the Publisher, except as permitted by U.S. copyright law. Address inquiries to Semper Memento Inc. 7558 W. Thunderbird Rd Ste 1 #442, Peoria, AZ 85381

Cover and book design by C Shepard
Interior images by C Shepard
http://www.aColumbineSite.com

Interior images by C Shepard.

Published by Overview Publishing.

Shepard, C.
 A Columbine book : who what where when why / C. Shepard.
 — First Edition
   p. cm.
 ISBN 979-8-9916221-1-0 (hc.)
 ISBN 979-8-9870778-9-4 (pbk.)
 ISBN 979-8-9916221-2-7 (ebook)

LCCN: 2024924669

PRINTED IN THE UNITED STATES OF AMERICA

10 9 8 7 6 5 4 3 2 1
First Edition

Dedicated to:

The Columbine families and faculty

Columbine Serves

Researchers, educators, and first responders everywhere

A COLUMBINE BOOK series by C Shepard:

- We Are All Columbine: 25 Years of Healing
- A Columbine Book: Who. What. When. Where. Why?

TABLE OF CONTENTS

25 YEARS…	1
- Past to future	3
- Columbine Day of Service	8
SETTING THE RECORD STRAIGHT	10
- Media confusion	11
- Official response	16
- Guerra report	18
- Basement Tapes	20
- Conspiracy theories & false information	23
AFTERMATH	39
- Zanis crosses	40
- NRA convention	41
- Back to school	42
- Lawsuits	45
LASTING IMPACT	48
- Crisis response	50
- Zero-tolerance	54
- Impact on media	56
- Change and lack thereof	60
- Rachel's Challenge	62
THE COLUMBINE FAMILIES	64
- Those who died	69
- The injured	85
- Uninjured survivors	106
COLUMBINE NOW	110
- Columbine staff	111
- April 20, 2024	115
MOVING FORWARD	123
- Path to healing	124
- Change for the future	129
- Your role	133
CONCLUSION	
-Final thoughts	136
REFERENCES & RESOURCES	139

25 YEARS...

Imagine your whole life being shaped around a single event.

Consider what you were before today. All the memories, the ups and downs, the life experiences you've had up until this point. Think of some of the key events you've gone through. Your first day of school. A memorable holiday or two. The first time you lost a friend, a family member, a pet. Your first crush. Your earliest successes. Your most embarrassing moments. The excitement of a birthday party or graduation. Your first real responsibility. Your best qualities and funniest quirks. Your hobbies and interests. Think about the plans you made for the future at various stages of your life. What did you dream of? Where did you want to go? What did you want to learn about? Who would you love to meet? What would you enjoy doing with your time if you could pick any career or pastime? What sort of legacy do you want to leave behind?

Now take all of that and throw it away.

Paint it over with a single terrible event that erases your identity outside of your relation to it. Whoever you were before is gone. Anything you used to be or wanted to become is now overshadowed by an awful moment completely beyond your control. You are now and forever a living embodiment of the event. That is your identity: The crisis you endured.

A COLUMBINE BOOK – WE ARE ALL COLUMBINE

That's the effect the shooting at Columbine High School had on many people who lived through it. One miserable day drastically altered their lives and permanently shaped their experience going forward. Even those who wished to live anonymous lives couldn't avoid it creeping back in, sometimes when least expected. For several, their entire existence was completely overwritten by the tragedy. Whatever they had been doing or intended to do with their lives was brutally derailed. On April 20, 1999, they stopped being a parent, a student, a teacher, a person… and became a facet of what happened.

Frank DeAngelis, the principal of Columbine High during the shooting, has become synonymous with the phrase "We are all Columbine". Craig Scott will always be the brother of slain victim Rachel Scott in the eyes of the public, the boy in the red shirt who survived a hail of gunfire in the library that killed the friends he hid with. Cassie Bernall will forever be known as the girl who said "yes", even though she didn't. The complex individual she was and could have been was blown away, replaced with the legacy of the martyr of Columbine.

Some survivors never got a chance to experience life outside the frame of the Columbine massacre, forever associated with the shooting in the public eye. Some have gone deep into hiding to try to escape the shadow of the horrific event, while others have learned to embrace their new identities and use them to push for positive change.

But we all reach a point where we want to move forward in life. To stop focusing on what's happened before and start looking to what comes next. For many people who lived through the tragic events of April 20, 1999, that time is now.

This book was written with the Columbine families in mind, to set the public record straight about several things that have troubled them and to show the world how they have taken their pain and turned it into something positive. It is about truth and healing and the road ahead.

PAST TO FUTURE

It's been 25 years since Columbine High School came to the attention of the public in a shocking series of news broadcasts. 25 years since two angry young men horrified the world with their devastating actions. 25 years of societal changes, global events, innovation, quarantine, backsliding and progress. The world truly is a different place than it was in 1999.

For the past quarter of a century, I have maintained a reference website online about the Columbine shooting: http://www.aColumbineSite.com. A Columbine Site, known informally to those who use it as the ACS, went up on the Internet on April 21, 1999. It was originally a one-page memorial to the as-yet-unnamed people who were killed and injured during the shocking tragedy. Watching the event unfold on live news evoked powerful emotions in me, both as someone with a recent upper middle-class high school background and as a young parent of a child who was nearing kindergarten age.

Like many who saw the gut-wrenching footage, witnessing it spurred me to want to do something—anything—to help. I wanted to understand what had happened and why. I had so many questions with no solid answers. How could I help? Who was involved? How many had died? What of the survivors? Who were their victims? Why? Who were the gunmen and why did they do what they did?

As that first week passed, I doggedly scoured the Web for an explanation or a few more details about the attack, but there was little information to be found anywhere. In 1999, newspapers were still a thing. News agencies were still locked on the idea that print was the best way to go, so most local news and newspaper websites didn't carry many headlines from outside of their state, if they existed at all. Most of the national sites posted updates only on a weekly basis. Same thing went for news magazines: Either they didn't have much of an online presence or they didn't update their sites often. There were a few exceptions to this, but those exceptions weren't helpful as they were parroting what the news broadcasts were saying.

And what the media was airing was sloppy reporting at best. Things that were aired were often speculation or sensationalized the situation. The news outlets were treating every rumor, interview, and forum post like it was researched truth. Without fact-checking, a massive amount of misinformation was reported as legitimate. To this day there is a mountain of unsubstantiated "facts" that are entirely wrong, lies, misconceptions, and conspiracy theories that are touted as solid truth.

Some of the misinformation put out there was intended to pull in an audience, while some came about simply because someone wanted to push a narrative for religious or personal reasons. Some of the misinformation was born from the confusion of the day. Other erroneous ideas came from hostile sources who were venting personal feelings taken as genuine fact by the reporters that heard them. Over the years, the memories of some survivors have faded or gotten confused, making them vulnerable to evangelists, authors, and reporters who took liberties with the details. Some of the false information will never be fully corrected because there are too many people who want the fake stories to be real.

Frustrated with the lack of honest, accurate documentation of the event and concerned that the real story would get lost, I started posting to my website the legitimate information I found. I researched day and night, digging deep and tapping resources I had in the Denver area to get ahold of newspapers and photos, and to be certain that what I was sharing was genuine. I worked with police, counselors, school officials, neighbors of Columbine High, the FBI, and even Scotland Yard to provide accurate information. I have actively tried to quash the spread of fake news and the glorification of the shooters and this tragic event while providing researchers with accurate information, and to help those who had to live through it by giving the public an unbiased source of their experiences to

25 YEARS...

reference. Many Columbine families have shared their dissatisfaction with the amount of misinformation out there. Those I've spoken with and have welcomed my attempts to set the record straight.

Over the years my site has become the most referenced online resource for dozens of books, magazine and news stories, websites, documentaries, educational plans, essays, and disaster readiness programs worldwide. Millions of people come to the site each year to find answers to questions the survivors really shouldn't have to keep answering or even deal with as they've tried to forge ahead in life. It's much easier to move forward if you're not constantly having to look back.

In 2024, I attended the 25th memorial service at Columbine High School with my friend and fellow author Sean Reavie, a highly decorated Phoenix police officer. He was invited there by School Resource Officer Eric Ebling. It was a private service, so I was honored to be included. Out of respect for the people who worked and attended school at Columbine, I had never gone to the property before. I was invited to the dedication of the Columbine Memorial on September 21, 2007, but was unable to attend due to the arrival of a new baby in my family. Getting to go to the 25th memorial felt like I was coming full circle with the website I started back in 1999.

On April 17th, 2024, the weather was a sunny 74 degrees Fahrenheit in Denver. On April 19th, the day Sean and I flew out to Colorado, the temperature dropped to 38 degrees. Flat gray clouds choked the skies. On our way to our hotel in the Ken Caryl neighborhood, snow began to fall. It reminded me of how it started to snow on April 21st, 1999, when the shooters' bodies were removed from the school. This was a bleak, unpleasant, slushy snowstorm that made driving a nervous experience. Snow was already piling up by the time we pulled into the parking lot of the hotel.

After settling into our rooms, we got ready to head back out into the unpleasant weather. The first thing we were scheduled to do was attend a gathering at the home of the School

Resource Officer who invited us. His house was in a quaint neighborhood just a few minutes away from the high school. The houses we passed strongly reminded me of the one the Harrises lived in back in 1999. It was a bit eerie driving through scenery I had only seen in photos up till then, knowing the old Harris house was just a couple of streets away.

When we arrived at his house, we were welcomed in by SRO Eric Ebling and his rescue dog, a large pup who was both timid and very interested in us. We chatted for a while, getting to know one another before he took us to where the main gathering was taking place. It had the feel of a house party, with bottles of fine whiskey and bourbon open on the counter. At one point, our host went to get something from the basement and again I was reminded of Columbine. In video footage I had seen recorded by Eric Harris and Dylan Klebold, they went down a surprisingly similar set of stairs to a basement while filming *Radioactive Clothing*.

There was Blackjack Pizza delivered, which was very tasty. Though there was a chain location in my hometown, I had never had it before. As we ate, we got to know those who were in attendance. Most of the people there were either students at Columbine during the shooting or faculty who'd been there. Some were now both. Everyone there had a connection to the shooting somehow, including myself and Sean.

My connection was through my website and the people I've met over the years because of it. Sean was brought into the loop through an interview he did with automotive legend Jon Moss for his book, *Keys to the Kingdom*. Through that interview he learned a great deal about John Tomlin, who was a Chevrolet truck enthusiast before his death in Columbine's library. You can read in Sean's book the touching story of what happened to John's truck after the makeshift memorials were cleared away. Sean and I are linked through the charity he founded that supports crisis centers for child victims of crime, founded when he was working as an officer in the Crimes Against Children unit. I've been a volunteer with this worthy cause since 2015.

25 YEARS...

Two wonderful gentlemen I spent the most time talking to were faculty members at Columbine during the shooting. They were still faculty there at the time of this writing. For the sake of their privacy, I have withheld their names as neither is interested in being a public face for the tragedy.

Our conversation was split between the serious subject of Columbine and more mundane interests, such as my friend's automotive book. Both men were car enthusiasts, and we talked at length about the various vehicles we loved. It was generally agreed that vintage sports cars were the best. Whenever the subject inevitably circled back around to Columbine, it was plain that though 25 years had passed, what they lived through was forever etched in their hearts and minds. The pain was still there, still fresh.

But there was also hope. Not just in them but everyone I spoke to that night. Everyone seemed to genuinely feel this year was different. A curtain had been lifted. There were better, brighter times coming in the legacy of Columbine for its survivors.

The general sentiment there and throughout the whole trip was that it was finally time to let the past be the past. It was time to stop looking back, to stop looking around, and start focusing on what lies ahead. Time to heal and grow and embrace the future. Enough time has been spent lingering in sorrow and confusion. They had arrived at a point where they wanted to stop being victimized by what happened and put all their energy into the positive things that were coming out of it. When CBS Colorado connected with the Columbine families, most agreed that they wanted the news agency to focus on the positive changes that have come from April 20th.

COLUMBINE DAY OF SERVICE

One place that positive energy is going is to the annual Columbine **Day of Service**.

The event was organized April 20, 2017, by many of the same people who have been key in other Columbine-centric initiatives such as the Columbine Memorial. The Day of Service project was started to benefit the community and bring some good to an otherwise dark day in Colorado. The event is affiliated with and supported by the United Way, Volunteers of America, and Habitat for Humanity. In 2019, Governor Jared Polis signed a decree that declared April 20th an official Day of Recommitment for Colorado, to "turn pain into healing and hatred into enlightenment and love".

Dawn Anna said in an interview with CBS News:

"We had a lot taken from us, but we had a lot given to us as well in the form of lots of open hearts and a lot of love and a lot of understanding. That's what we are trying to give back on that day."

Whether it's donating time or supplies, or simply reading to someone, the Day of Service is intended to put some much-needed love out there. Not only to honor the lives lost and observe how everyone's lives were forever changed, but also to make a positive impact on the community.

The idea isn't just for the families of Columbine, either, or Colorado. It has become an outreach to all communities worldwide who wish to engage. The group encourages others through their website (https://www.columbineserves.org/) to create a global movement by supporting those who have experienced tragedy. To turn something bad into ongoing good.

In 2023, the Day of Service generated over 60 projects in 6 states and 10 countries. It's a movement that will surely continue to gain traction in the future. In 2024, Columbine alone organized over 40 projects. 44 of the 47 they had scheduled went

25 YEARS...

off as planned despite the snowstorm, including a food drive and remodeling Habitat for Humanity homes. In 2017, roughly 400 students volunteered. In 2024, over 1,200 students and 65 faculty were involved at Columbine. In addition to the Columbine community's local projects, there were at least 40 more projects that happened in California, Illinois, Nebraska, Arizona, Canada, Indonesia, and Russia. Columbine even received a message of support from a research station in Antarctica. The Day of Service is a movement that highlights the positive things that can come in the wake of tragedy and will surely continue to gain traction in the future.

April is Global Volunteer Month. In 2024, April 21-27 was National Volunteer Week. The first National Volunteer Week was in 1974, so this year commemorated the 50th anniversary of the observation. The core idea is to recognize the impact of volunteer service. It shines a light on the people who inspire us to serve. Columbine's Day of Service has helped the community reclaim April 20th and turn it into a world-wide call to action, to inspire positive change everywhere.

SETTING THE RECORD STRAIGHT

The first hours and days after the shooting were confused, chaotic, stressful, and agonizing. The shooting was unprecedented. Nothing of its scale had been managed by law enforcement, the media, or the public. There were no protocols that applied, no script to follow. Moment by moment the event played out, with everyone waiting anxiously for any solid information. This was hardest on the families who lost loved ones, most of whom had to wait for days before they had confirmation that their child had been killed. Recovering from that has been a healing process beyond that of dealing with the loss of a child. Each family and individual have dealt with it in their own ways.

Since the start there has been a staggering amount of misinformation that plagues the details of this event. Some of the most popular books and documentary films about the subject contain glaring errors that feed public confusion about what happened. While this book is by no means all-inclusive, I have tried to address some of the most prominent examples that need correcting. I have specifically focused on subjects that were either the most harmful to understanding the nature of this event or subjects that the Columbine families have expressed an interest in seeing corrected. No disrespect is intended toward any individuals or agencies. This is strictly about setting the record straight. Every attempt has been made to provide honest, unbiased, and validated information.

SETTING THE RECORD STRAIGHT

MEDIA CONFUSION

On April 20th, 1999, there were several media vans in the neighborhood near Columbine High, manned by reporters who were on the trail of the JonBenét Ramsey murder. Some of the journalists got wind of the shooting via the police scanner and, with nothing else to do, it wasn't long before a whole flock of news teams descended on the school looking for a scoop of the action. They were so anxious to be on scene, some even drove up onto the grass and parked there, which made it difficult for first responders to get in close to the school. Yet despite their enthusiasm to report on the developing story, they got many things wrong.

COLUMBINE WASN'T LITTLETON

Journalists seeking more information about the shooting at Columbine High used the Internet to dig up the school's address. This is where confusion in the media regarding Littleton as the location of the event began.

Columbine High School is situated in the Columbine area, which is an unincorporated community in southern Jefferson County. As such, the school has a postal address in Littleton, the nearest incorporated city with federal postal service. Littleton is in Arapahoe County. Littleton Fire Department services the school and were among some of the first responders to the scene that day.

When reporters searched for the school and saw the postal address, they seized on it. They called everyone in Littleton they could in the hopes of getting even a few crumbs of information. Columbine is in Jefferson County. They called Littleton Mayor Pat Cronenberger. Even the historical museum in Littleton received calls from people who were wildly hoping they could contact an official within the government there to talk to. Every agency they called tried to correct them but even after they were made aware of their mistake, the media continued to report the location of the shooting was Littleton. The name has become permanently linked to the tragedy because of it.

24 HOURS OF CONFUSION

The assault on Columbine was the first mass shooting event that was televised, and mistakes were made in the way reporting was handled. There were three 24-hour news networks on television (MSNBC, CNN, and Fox) at the time and they were broadcasting Columbine around the clock. With law enforcement treating the scene like a hostage situation, there was plenty of time for the news agencies to take pictures and stage interviews. However, there wasn't much solid information to be had which led to speculation and rumor being treated as fact. In the rush to get the story out, misinformation was passed off as fact by the media. Every radio station and news show were saying something different. The number of victims and gunmen varied hourly. Who the people involved were and why it happened also varied depending on the broadcasting station.

The first live news reports covering the shooting started around a half hour after the first shots were fired on the campus. Reporters were some of the first people the survivors spoke to once they made it out of the school. Before they could give statements to officers, several kids fresh from the line of fire faced microphones and cameras thrust at them by eager newshounds asking questions the traumatized teens didn't have the answers to. News anchors showed up at the triage sites and badgered city officials over the phone, pressing for more information. Some even showed up at hospitals where the injured were undergoing surgery, and on the doorsteps of the families of the victims asking invasive questions and, in some cases, spreading false information about the victims. They clipped and edited interviews, boiling down hours of footage to suit the narratives they wanted to push.

SETTING THE RECORD STRAIGHT

REVENGE OF THE NERDS SPIN

Despite the tremendous amount of footage recorded, the focus of most news reports was the gunmen. The media's attention was on the mystery of the shooters and not on the people they harmed or the impact it had on the community. Without meaning to, the media networks sensationalized the killers. It was all about them: Who they were, what their motives were, what they wore and who they knew.

They were initially portrayed as sympathetic, awkward underdogs who had retaliated against those who had bullied them. This "revenge of the nerds" narrative polarized early opinions of the situation before any solid facts were established. No one even knew who the victims were yet, let alone what their relationships to the gunmen were. The idea of picked-on underdogs striking back was an idea people could relate to, which made it easy to believe.

Over time the true horror of the situation came to light. Disturbing essays and websites that the gunmen wrote were discovered. Police reports surfaced. People who knew them came forward with stories of their antisocial and dangerous behavior in the weeks that preceded the massacre. Then the Basement Tapes were leaked, wherein the shooters projected a vicious air of superiority as they boasted about how they were going to indiscriminately kill as many people as they could – even their own friends.

As more details emerged over the following weeks and news agencies shifted the focus of their stories to the victims and their families. But by then the "underdog" narrative was pounded into public conscience so thoroughly that the misinformation in those first broadcasts was almost impossible to retract or correct. Fixating on the killers made them the main characters in the tragedy, adding a level of glory to what they did which copycats later seized on.

MEDIA CIRCUS

By Wednesday the 21st, the day after the shootings, news trucks from all over the nation were parked around Columbine High. Cables snaked across the ground in all directions and pop-up tents stood ready to shelter reporters from the cold rain. After the bomb squads finished sweeping the property, Jefferson County (JeffCo) Sheriff's Office pulled the police lines in closer to the school. The media immediately crowded in for the best shots they could get of the building and grounds. Before the sun rose, they began taping interviews with survivors, their families, and the families of kids who were injured and killed. While Bree Pasquale was interviewed by the *Today* show, the parents of victim Dan Rohrbough were being interviewed by *Good Morning America*. On Thursday, the area looked like a street festival. Network tents stood in rows while journalists and photographers circled Clement Park, recording mourners as they brought tributes to makeshift memorials scattered around the park. No quiet moments of reflection could be found with so many agencies seeking more content for their broadcasts.

Police investigation began immediately. As soon as officials knew the suspects' identities, they began questioning people and searching off-campus locations. The shooters' friends were detained while news cameras rolled. The Klebolds and the Harrises had to leave their homes because their houses were considered crime scenes and closed by investigators. The families found it difficult to find someplace to go where they wouldn't be harassed by the media and the public. Even after they were allowed to return to their homes, they found curious onlookers and reporters hiding on their property, waiting for any new development.

The Stair family faced a similar problem. Joseph Stair was a former Trench Coat Mafia member whom the media fixated on. Although he graduated the previous year and hadn't seen the gunmen in several months, journalists hounded Joe's family. The misinformation they ran with implicated Joe and his friends and drew negative attention to the family. In addition to

SETTING THE RECORD STRAIGHT

the media swarm, they had to deal with death threats from people who were eager to find any place to direct their agitated emotions at. The Stairs eventually had to leave the phone off the hook to avoid the inundation.

Joe's sister Amanda told Westword in 2019: *"People were latching on to the first thing they heard and wanted to be the first to report it, whether it was true or not."*

Other members of the Trench Coat Mafia were accused of having something to do with the shooting or having foreknowledge of it, which eventually prompted some to attend a televised press conference where they denied involvement and extended heartfelt sympathies to the victims and their families.

Not all the media attention was unwelcome, though. Some survivors and parents felt the footage of them during those vulnerable moments was something the public needed to witness, to understand how horrible the situation was. Student Bree Pasquale was threatened by one of the gunmen in the library. She was one of the first survivors interviewed, giving her statement to the media just minutes after the shooter pointed a gun at her head. She believed the raw truth of her immediate reaction was important for the world to see. Footage of her anguished description of the terrifying experience replayed on KUSA, CNN, and NBC, driving their ratings up to record-breaking numbers.

The scrutiny paid to the scene was so intense, even members of the press grew uneasy with how intrusive they were being. Alicia Acuña of Fox News said: *"Sometimes it's hard to listen. You're torn between wondering if it's best for them to talk and doing your job. There's a certain type of exploitation."*

Photographers on the scene later described how they adopted a sort of "war time" mentality complete with gallows humor to protect themselves from the images they were capturing in their 12-hour days of snapping pictures. And while that method worked initially, some found themselves quickly questioning their intrusion into the suffering of others. Was it really worth it to "get the picture"?

OFFICIAL RESPONSE

The official response to the shooting was widely criticized for being too slow, and for taking the wrong approach to the situation. The insistence of chain of command on the part of the SWAT frustrated everyone, from the victims to the first responders on the scene. Police officers who had been there from the start were forced to stand down and watch while the gunmen terrorized the school because there was no established protocol for such an event. Command defaulted to a standard "wait and secure" method devised following the clock tower shooting in Texas in 1966. The event was treated like a hostage situation, which meant waiting for demands that weren't coming. Instead, the slow approach gave the gunmen all the time they wanted to kill whoever they felt like.

The "wait and secure" method failed the people officials were supposed to protect that day. Law enforcement on campus could see it was failing and resented being sidelined. More than one officer there had a child inside the school at the time. Several discussed breaking rank and going in anyway. Principal Frank DeAngelis was in a similar boat: He had been actively evacuating students, trying to save as many lives as he could. When he emerged with a gaggle of kids after the official perimeter was established, he was stopped, held back from reentering the building. It was torture for him to stand outside listening to the bombs and gunfire, unable to do anything to protect the kids he cared about who he knew were in mortal danger.

With over 1,000 law enforcement personnel on the scene, official radio channels were snarled up with dozens of authorities all trying to report at once. Coordinating and making sense of the chatter on various channels was a logistical nightmare for the overwhelmed dispatchers. First responders from all over the Denver metro area came to the scene only to wade into confusion as no one knew where they were supposed to go. Officers who arrived first covered the entrances, many of them operating without body armor as they dodged bullets and provided cover fire for people fleeing the school. Some officials were unarmed, unable to do more to help than transport victims away from the scene. Ambulance drivers and EMTs wound up in the line of fire as they received no information that the crime scene was still active. The arrival of superior officers and the assembly and mobilization of SWAT teams slowed things down further as they took control of the scene.

Frustrated with the agonizing wait, officers with Principal DeAngelis had him describe the layout of the building for them. They provided him with a small whiteboard to draw a map on as the blueprints they were working from predated reconstruction that was done in 1995. They even floated the notion of putting the principal in a bullet-proof vest so he could guide them. The idea was denied by superior officers.

Inside, the fire alarms continued to blare for hours because the fire department couldn't get in to turn them off. And while armored units did eventually make it to the scene, the officers on site had to utilize everything from a fire truck to a construction vehicle as defense to get in close to the school. Neither of those machines was suited to the wet, uneven terrain outside Columbine High.

As Coach Dave Sanders lay bleeding to death on the floor of a science classroom, students and teachers with him desperately did everything they could to try to get someone in to save him. It took hours for help to make it to the room he was in. By then it was too late. That alone drew massive amounts of criticism from the public and wrongful death lawsuits from Sanders' family.

Other families sued Jefferson County as well, stating that the event and loss of life wouldn't have been as bad if the officials on scene had moved in quicker and taken stronger action. The Harrises and Klebolds were named in other lawsuits, as was Columbine, for failing to recognize the threat Eric and Dylan presented. The large collection of evidence that surfaced in the days following the shootings painted a picture in retrospect of disaster waiting to happen. But no one person held all the clues.

No one person saw everything that went into the dangerous concoction that resulted in the tragedy.

But that doesn't account for the sheer number of problems the subsequent investigation had afterward. Reports, interviews, and tapes went missing or were never recorded. Evidence was destroyed, sometimes in secret. Official timelines didn't line up. Crucial tests were never conducted. Investigators lied or were mistaken about information they gave to the families, or they produced it too slowly to be of help to the courts. The ongoing issues led many people, even other government agencies, to scrutinize the event, the investigations and the official reports, with several suspecting conspiracies and/or cover-ups. Families of the victims called for independent investigation and were assisted by agencies such as the El Paso County Sheriff's Office.

COMMUNITY GRATITUDE TO RESPONDERS

Though there were major issues with the way the shooting was handled during and after the event, the Columbine community and the individuals directly affected were and are grateful to the men and women who struggled through hours of stress and uncertainty to help them. Among those regarded as heroes in the eyes of the survivors are the faculty who helped get people out of harm's way, and the fire department, EMTs, and deputies who risked being shot to help save lives.

GUERRA REPORT

The Brown family dealt with a great deal of stress from the fallout from the Columbine shooting, due in part to the way some of the official documents were handled. One specific matter had to do with the report Judy and Randy made to the police in March 1998 about a web blog posted by Eric Harris that he wrote in 1997 which threatened their son Brooks Brown.

SETTING THE RECORD STRAIGHT

Brooks had been friends with Harris until a fight about rides to school caused a rift between them. After Brown was alerted to the website on March 17, 1998, by Dylan Klebold he told his parents about it. After seeing the threatening rants and their phone number and home address posted, they decided to talk to the police. On March 18, they gave Detective Mark Miller the web addresses to begin the investigation. On March 26, 1998, the case was closed without ever having been assigned to an investigator. The Browns were not notified of the closure.

On March 31st, the Browns met with Investigator Mike Guerra (a former SRO at Columbine), Detective Glenn Grove, and Deputy John Hicks. The Browns were not aware that their case had already been closed. At the time of their report, Guerra was looking into case #3365, a report of an unexploded pipe bomb that was found 2-3 miles from the Harris home. He suspected it might be tied to information about the bombs Eric Harris says on his website that he made. Guerra worked on the case for 3-4 days, during which found Harris' "shit list" of people he wanted to see die. Guerra also discovered Eric's hate-filled rants and notes about the bombs he and Dylan had been making. In the process of the investigation, a computer check turned up arrest reports for Eric Harris and Dylan Klebold having to do with their breaking into a van that January. Both Guerra and Hicks saw it, however Jefferson County officials would later insist that computer checks of records didn't turn up anything having to do with the prior arrest of the shooters.

Guerra wrote an affidavit for a search warrant for the Harris house, but a District Attorney told him there was no probable cause. So, the warrant wasn't filed, and nothing came of the complaint. In the months that followed the shootings, the Guerra Documents and daily log sheets disappeared. They remained missing for several years.

The Guerra documents were eventually found in a three-ring binder that was unrelated to the investigation. A grand jury inquiry into the matter was launched in 2004. In the official statement that followed, the grand jury stated that it *"cannot determine whether the absence of all original official records, any handwritten notes, the complete working file and all electronic documents is tied to a particular person or the result of a particular crime."*

Randy Brown declared it collusion and a criminal conspiracy.

His son Brooks Brown has faced public criticism due to his association with the gunmen prior to the shootings and the fact that he was one of the last individuals to speak with Eric Harris, just minutes before the shooting started. Some people have suggested that he might know more than he has let on over the years. Some have gone as far as to accuse him of having something to do with the shooting. The finger of blame has also been leveled at the parents of the gunmen, members of the Trench Coat Mafia, and others. It's impossible to say what anyone who knew the shooters might have known about their intentions before the fact. All we can do is deal with what we know for sure. Healing comes from letting go of speculation if it doesn't help resolve anything.

BASEMENT TAPES

Among the evidence collected in the wake of the Columbine shooting were several videos made by Eric Harris, Dylan Klebold, and their friends. Spread across five VHS tapes, some of the videos included fictional shorts, school projects and screenplays recorded just for fun. Others were video blogs of the young men testing their weapons on a firing range. The worst videos were of the gunmen showing off their arsenal, and ones where they raged and ranted in Harris' basement about how they wanted to hurt and kill people.

The videos, called the "Basement Tapes" by the media, were confiscated from the Harris home, from the Audio/Video lab at Columbine, and from Eric Veik, a student who helped the gunmen with several of their projects. Veik had some of the tapes

SETTING THE RECORD STRAIGHT

in his backpack on the morning of the shooting. He had plans to edit them for A/V class with Harris later that day. Thinking the alarms in the hall were just a drill, he followed protocol and left his backpack behind in his classroom, believing he would be back soon to retrieve it. When interviewed by investigators, he told them about the videos and where to find his backpack. They confiscated the bag and the tapes.

All the tapes were marked as evidence items. Investigators viewed them and then stowed them with the other evidence. The tapes were kept in the vaults until the Jefferson County Sheriff's Office made the questionable decision to allow access to the tapes to *TIME* reporter Tim Roche. With permission of the Sheriff's Office, Kate Battan, a lead investigator in the Columbine massacre, let the journalist view segments of the tapes (though not the full 3+ hours of footage) to give him a better understanding of Klebold and Harris and their plans.

After viewing the tapes, Roche wrote a lengthy article for *TIME* magazine entitled "The Columbine Tapes", wherein he included direct quotes from the videos. The issue hit newsstands on December 20, 1999, emblazoned with an image of Harris and Klebold in the cafeteria taken from the security cameras as they tried to detonate one of the propane bombs. The article came as a shock to the families of the victims, who didn't know about the tapes and hadn't been offered a chance to view them.

Brian Rohrbough, father of victim Daniel, told the media in an interview: *"I'm at a loss to see what good this story was going to bring to the community or to the rest of us two weeks before Christmas."*

Dale Todd, father of injured survivor Evan Todd, denounced the videos as "disgusting".

Undersheriff John Dunaway claimed Roche never told him he was going to write an article about the tapes. He said that the journalist was given permission by Sheriff John Stone to view the abridged material because Roche made it seem as though he wanted to write an article about the investigation and official response of the SWAT during the attack. He also claimed Roche violated a confidentiality agreement by publishing portions of the tapes in the article. *TIME*'s spokesperson Diana Pearson countered that claim, stating there was no such agreement in place, nor did the Sheriff's Office ask Roche to not to report on the content of the tapes. Dunaway said that Roche never would have been allowed access to the tapes if officials knew he planned to refer to them in his article.

Days later, JeffCo allowed a small handful of reporters for other news agencies to view the tapes. In response to questions about the rationale behind allowing the press to view the tapes, Wayne Halverson, a spokesman for the Sheriff's Office, said it was done because authorities were afraid that only one media outlet for the information had "potential for sensationalism and the resulting anguish to the victims' families." Around that time, some audio from the tapes was also leaked and played on news reports. The sound clips only circulated for a couple of days before stations stopped airing them.

After the scandalous leaks, some of the Columbine families pushed to be allowed access to the footage that was shared with the journalists. Dan Rohrbough's mother Sue Petrone wanted to see the abridged footage that the reporter did. She said to reporters that she knew it would set her back in her progress toward healing, but it was something she needed to see and process. She wanted to hear from the killers themselves what they were thinking.

After some resistance and legal action from the families, JeffCo allowed them to view the excerpts from the tapes. Randy Brown insisted on seeing them though he was initially told he wouldn't be allowed to. The Harrises and Klebolds were also allowed to view the footage. All the families were given the option to either go to the sheriff's office or to view the videos in their own homes. Each family's response was different. Some didn't want to see them at all. Victim Valeen Schnurr was angry at the shooters until she saw the footage. She said at that point she let go of her anger. She could see how mentally ill they were.

SETTING THE RECORD STRAIGHT

Investigator Kate Battan was with the shooters' families when they viewed what their sons had recorded. The Klebolds surprised Battan by asking to come to the office. At the time, members of the press were avidly stalking the officials. The family brought two or three lawyers with them. Battan told them that during the viewing they could take breaks if they needed to. They sat there stoically through the whole thing. According to Battan, neither parent showed much emotion while watching the footage. At the end of the nearly 3-hour hate-filled video, Tom Klebold turned to the investigator and stunned her by saying:

"See? He didn't want to do this."

The Harrises requested a viewing at their home. They had their personal lawyer and a therapist with them. They took a lot of breaks, so many that Battan was at their house all evening. They held each other, crying, and when they called for a break, they went into a bedroom with their therapist for several minutes. When they returned, they apologized profusely to the investigator. It was Battan's impression that both families care about the victims and their families.

Over the years, Sue Klebold has come forward to offer public apologies and empathy toward them. The Harrises disappeared. Battan said that the family quickly moved out of the country when they could.

CONSPIRACY THEORIES & FALSE INFORMATION

The weeks following the shooting were filled with confused disinformation being reported as fact. False information was fed to investigators, families, and the public by various sources. Some were just conspiracy theories born from too little information. Others were deliberate cover-ups or distortions of what happened. In some cases, fake news was cooked up by people who wanted attention or closure to the tragic event. Some were more devious: Denials of what happened, rewriting of facts, outright lies and malicious rumormongering plagued the investigation.

This has been the case since the beginning. News outlets and journalists put out versions of what happened that were later proven to be untrue. And while there have been several authors and filmmakers who have tried to correct the inaccuracies that have been accepted by the masses, it's an uphill battle that can never be won. Especially when there are people out there actively trying to subvert the truth and twist it to suit their own purposes.

Conspiracy theories about Columbine cover a wide range: Some promote the idea that the event was a government exercise or intense coverup, while others go so far as to claim that the whole thing was fabricated to scare people. More niche conspiracies involve a third gunman or whether the gunmen truly committed suicide.

Some misguided individuals idealize the killers. Groups of criminal theorists and self-described fans of true crime post speculative rants online about the personalities and agendas of the shooters. There are even websites where people roleplay together as the gunmen or write fan fiction about them, turning them into love interests or misunderstood heroes. Beyond the obvious inappropriateness of turning real people into fictional romance characters, this sort of play-acting has led some individuals to believe their fiction represents the "real" identities of the killers. They ingrain their fantasy versions of these people in their imaginations until the reality is lost.

A need for acceptance drives some of this behavior. Other misguided individuals believe the aggression and pain they feel is justified if they can shape the perpetrators into someone more like them, or someone they could have been friends with. It's a self-deception that typically sorts itself out as a person matures or when they put true effort and empathy into understanding how the event impacted the victims. Some may continue to defend their fictionalizing of the killers. It can be difficult for a person to acknowledge when they're wrong, especially if their opinion is directly tied to their view of themselves.

COLUMBINE WAS (NOT) A HOAX

There is a psychological effect known as "psychic numbing" wherein the larger a traumatic event is, the less likely we are to view the people involved as people. A point is reached where we don't hear enough about the people who were impacted to connect with them. That was part of the problem with the media focusing on the shooters: They became relatable people while their victims were just numbers.

Beyond that, though, there is a type of conspiracy theorist out there who believes news-worthy tragedies aren't real but are instead staged events. Whether this stems from a need for the world to be safe or an inability to accept that bad things can happen on a broad scale is unclear. Psychologists and sociologists continue to study this phenomenon. It's generally agreed that humans by nature want easy explanations for what happens around us and things like mass shootings are difficult to explain. Rather than make sense of the complex puzzle, some prefer to deny it completely.

The level of denial can reach incredible proportions, spanning COVID and the Holocaust. Alex Jones was a radio shock jock who gained infamy after he spent months trying to convince others that the Las Vegas country music festival shooting and Sandy Hook school shooting weren't real. His arguments about Sandy Hook were so vicious and harmful, the families of the victims won a $1.5 billion lawsuit against him.

One of the strangest arguments among tragedy deniers came from a website that was written to support the flawed notion that Columbine was a staged hoax. The author's strongest point of contention was the claim that there were no people crying that day. The writer selected carefully curated images of people at the scene and pointed out that you couldn't see any tears. The people were making crying faces, the author said, but there were no tears visible.

Not only is this patently untrue—there are a multitude of photos and video footage where people can plainly be seen crying, complete with tears—but the images the author chose to fixate on were poor quality, long shots. Tears on human skin don't leave much evidence even if you're face to face with them. Trying to see them on a small, grainy digital image that's over 20 years old is virtually impossible. That same site featured a photo they claimed was of a victim who was shot, but there was no blood to be seen. So, obviously the event was a hoax. But the author didn't do their research: The photo they were complaining about was of an entirely different person than they said.

The worst of the disinformation out there was fed to families and to the investigators by people who weren't even involved in the tragic event. Conspiracy theories and other fake information have gotten so deeply rooted in the history of the event, it's easy for researchers to mistake it for fact. This section tackles some of the most notorious claims and theories, and who started them.

ROHRBOUGH (NOT) KILLED BY FRIENDLY FIRE

Daniel Rohrbough's family was put through avoidable stress and suffering due to a fabricated story Arapahoe County Deputy James "Jim" Taylor told them. He said their son had been killed by friendly fire. Taylor was a trusted, long-time friend of the family. When he told them he saw fellow officer Dan O'Shea shoot and kill Dan, they believed him. Taylor reiterated the story several times. It has been suggested that Taylor also told the same story to O'Shea a day or two after the shooting. Rohrbough's family believed the narrative completely and even started legal action against Jefferson County and Dan O'Shea on December 26, 2001.

SETTING THE RECORD STRAIGHT

On December 30, 2001, Arapahoe County Sheriff Pat Sullivan disputed the claim with a four-page written statement from Deputy Taylor in which he claimed he never said anything of the sort. Taylor denied being on the south side of the school where Dan Rohrbough was killed. In the written statement, Taylor said:

"Regarding being a witness to the Columbine shooting and standing next to a Denver officer while he shot—that is not true—the only things that were stated to Rohrbough family by me was seen on TV or reported in the newspaper. I'm sorry for their loss. It is not true that I saw Daniel Rohrbough get shot or any other person."

The Rohrboughs were stunned by the denial. Fortunately, Dan's mother Sue Petrone and her husband Rich recorded Taylor on one of the occasions where he told them this false tale. The family started recording all conversations about Columbine when they suspected they were being lied to by investigators. They presented the tape as evidence. On it, Taylor can be heard saying to them:

"What I seen was a boy coming down the sidewalk, you know. Kind of running, you know, a fast trot, but there was 20 or 30 other kids around, you know. I don't even know the number. They were just running in mass chaos, and I seen a boy drop and that's... and that's... I don't know who it was."

When Rich Petrone asked him if the boy was Dan, Taylor responded:

"It was Dan. And I didn't know that until I seen the photo the next morning in the newspaper that it was the boy that I seen."

Dan's father Brian Rohrbough contended that Taylor told him a similar story on April 21, 1999, the day after the shooting. When addressing Taylor's denial of the lies, the Rohrboughs' lawyer Barry Arrington pointed to the fact that when Taylor first told others this version of events, ballistics for the shooting hadn't even been started. There was no way he could have known who killed Daniel. Sheriff Sullivan verified that Taylor was stationed on the east side of the school, over a block away from the school, and could not have witnessed Rohrbough being shot.

In a meeting with internal affairs in January 2002, Taylor admitted to inspector Grant Reed that he had in fact lied to the family. His excuse was that he got "too emotionally overloaded" and had been "trying to console the family" and "help with the grieving" by claiming he had been in the middle of gunfire. Taylor told investigators:

"I never stopped to take a look at the whole big picture of what this was doing. At the time, I didn't realize I was being untruthful. Unfortunately, it sounds like this has totally misled the family, and that was not my intention at all."

Sullivan fired Taylor two days later.

There was initial confusion over which gunman killed Rohrbough. The Columbine Report states that it was Dylan Klebold who fired the fatal shot but an independent investigation by the El Paso County Sheriff's Department determined that Rorhbough died from a shot fired by Eric Harris, but it was never made clear whether Rorhbough was hit in the crossfire by law enforcement. In September of 2002, Dan Rohrbough's family sued Taylor for defamation, negligence, and outrageous behavior. The suit settled in 2003.

DEPOOTER (WAS NOT) IN HOSPITAL

For hours after the shooting, families were left hanging around Leawood Elementary, waiting as bus after bus dropped off frazzled, traumatized students. Each busload brought tearful reunions for some families, and more anxiety for others. It was so stressful a wait, one parent suffered heart trouble that required an ambulance.

SETTING THE RECORD STRAIGHT

As the hours ground on and afternoon became night, the last of the buses stopped coming. Hope wasn't entirely lost, though. There were many people in hospitals who were yet to be identified. Many of the injured weren't found with ID cards on them, so there was still a chance that a missing child was in surgery or recovery, alive but unable to communicate who they were to doctors.

Some of the families tried to go home. Some stayed, unwilling to abandon the one spot where they had hope of seeing their child again. By then, reporters were hounding everyone they could for details about the shooting. One called up the DePooter family. Their son Corey was among the missing unaccounted for. The reporter told them that Corey's name was on a hospital list. The DePooters anxiously called all the hospitals, but Corey wasn't in any of them.

STEPHANIE MUNSON (WAS NOT) IN PHOTO

The conspiracy theory mentioned earlier about the photo of a victim who was supposedly shot but had no visible injury is a favorite of many tragedy deniers. The author of that website and other people have singled out the photo of four girls fleeing the school that was featured on the cover of a May 1999 *Newsweek* magazine. They assumed the girl who looked the most agonized was Stephanie Munson, who was shot in the foot while escaping the school. This case of mistaken identity might have come from the fact that the girl in the photo appears to be leaning on her friends from support. Which she was – but her need for support was due to emotional trauma, not physical injury.

The girl in the famous photo taken by Kevin Higley of the Associated Press is Jessica Holliday, who was in the library during the shootings. Holliday was not injured but had just witnessed the murders of several people, some of whom were her friends. The girl to her left is Diwata Perez, who was under the library table where Lauren Townsend was killed. Both girls can be seen in another famous photo taken that day by George

Kochaniec. That picture became iconic of the shooting, wherein Holliday is gripping her head and sobbing to the sky while Perez stands to her left, injured and distraught.

There were no photos taken of Stephanie Munson until after treatment for her injury.

THIRD GUNMAN

One of the many conspiracy theories that cropped up early on and has stayed rooted in the subject of the Columbine tragedy was that of a third gunman. This started primarily because of two things: First was the presence of A/C repairman Chris Clark on the roof of the school during the shooting. The second was witness testimony.

Clark worked for ECS HVAC and was out on a service call to fix a leak above the girls' locker room. When the shooting started, he barricaded the access hatch and hid behind the air conditioning units to avoid being hit by shrapnel from the pipe bombs the gunmen threw onto the roof. He tried at one point to lower himself to the ground but the thin yellow rope he had with him wouldn't hold his weight, so he was stuck on the roof until he was rescued at 12:11 p.m.

Several individuals interviewed by the authorities gave conflicting statements about what the gunmen looked like. They had brown hair, blond hair, black hair. They wore all black or wore masks. One individual said she believed there was a third person shooting in the library because of how fast the shots were fired. What the shooters wore changed over the course of the attack, which made it more difficult to get solid descriptions. The gunmen started off wearing trench coats and wrap-around sunglasses. They each added a single fingerless glove to their outfits. They both removed their coats at different times. At some points they were carrying bags and backpacks while other times they had set those down to make moving about easier.

SETTING THE RECORD STRAIGHT

The subject of the number of participants has been scrutinized by independent researchers who decided information in the Columbine Report didn't seem to add up. In a short amount of time on April 20, 1999, Eric Harris and Dylan Klebold were supposedly seen in the parking lot of the bowling alley, at a gas station, in the parking lot of Columbine, and they recorded their farewell video. They set bombs in the cafeteria. How could they do all that and still have time to set up two diversionary explosives outside of the high school?

There is also the matter of the cafeteria bombs: Two devices were seen on security footage in the commons. This was verified by the Federal Bureau of Investigation (FBI) lab in Quantico, Virginia. A third undetonated 20-pound propane bomb was found in the kitchen during a sweep on Thursday, April 22. There is no footage of any of the bombs being placed as the cameras were offline from 11:14 a.m. to 11:22 a.m. It is unknown how the shooters got them into the school in that time. While some believe the kitchen device may have been placed there during the homecoming dance (the lock on the outer door had been tampered with that weekend), others think that someone else must have helped them on the morning of the shooting.

Witness statements from people outside placed a vehicle that looked like one Brooks Brown once owned at the scene. Though he had sold the vehicle, a parent who regularly drove by the area claimed to see a group of kids that morning in trench coats standing around a vehicle parked near the school. That vehicle matched the car's description. The witness said the teens were looking into the trunk of the car. A student at Columbine said they saw a similar vehicle race from the parking lot just before the attack. Yet another student witness said they saw someone in a trench coat and mask at one entrance of the school take off running across the parking lot as the shooting began. There was also an alleged discrepancy about the clothing Chris Morris was seen wearing at school that morning, the clothes he was arrested in, and the clothes that his brother surrendered to the authorities.

Ballistics from the scene show only Eric Harris, Dylan Klebold, and the authorities fired shots there. The security camera footage backs this up. Some have suggested that there may not have been a third shooter, but that the gunmen had help from their like-minded friends—the same people they did "missions" with and joked around with about shooting people. But whether they had help is a question that cannot be answered. If they did have assistance, those who helped them aren't going to be bragging about it. What anyone knew or suspected before and during the shooting will likely always be up for debate.

BRENDA PARKER AND MIKE SMITH LIES

One odd thing that happens with high profile crimes is how many people come forward claiming to have something to do with them when they didn't. People get caught up in the drama and make ridiculous claims. A couple of months after the shooting I received an email from someone who found my website who claimed to be best friends with Isaiah Shoels. "I called her Izzy," they said while lamenting the loss. I traced the email to a middle school student email address in Florida. Realizing the individual was likely under the age of 14 and was obviously upset about things, I told them as gently as I could that I understood their feelings on the matter, but that I knew they weren't a student at Columbine and told them Isaiah was a boy, not a girl. I never heard back from them.

Reporters and investigators both received calls and emails from people who pretended to be involved. Officials had to follow up on every false lead they received. News agencies weren't as thorough, often reporting everything they heard as fact without tracking down the source. One such example was a fellow who claimed to be a student at Columbine who was there during the shooting. He turned out to be a 25-year-old snowboarder from Utah. Other people who wanted attention to help them cope with their feelings about the shooting stuck to making their claims on the Internet through forums, chat rooms, and bulletin boards. The anonymity the Web afforded them meant they could claim just about anything without risk of getting called out for lying or getting in trouble with authorities.

Brenda Parker was one of the individuals who sought Internet clout by telling people online that she had connections to the shooting. Investigators contacted Parker in July 1999 after receiving a report that she was online claiming to have known gunman Eric Harris. (Columbine Report pages 10843-10851)

When she spoke with officials, Parker claimed that she was shopping with a friend at a Denver mall in January 1998 when Eric Harris and Dylan Klebold started following them around. According to her initial statement to the authorities, they all started chatting and she agreed to meet Harris the next day. She claimed they started seeing each other regularly and would go cruising in her Mustang. Supposedly they would go to where he worked at Blackjack Pizza where he would get her free food. They supposedly went bowling together and he helped her with her computer. She told investigators that she stopped seeing him when she found out he was 17 as she was 23 at the time. She also claimed to have called him in February 1999 to see how he was doing. She said that he was quiet and unfriendly and didn't seem like he had before. She provided a photo and a voice recording she claimed were of Harris, but investigators noted in their report that neither resembled any of the pictures or recordings they already had of Harris. She also told investigators that she had met Brooks Brown through Harris and had called Brown in July 1999 to see how he was doing. She said that she spent July 18 and 19 with him, but that they didn't talk about Columbine or the shooters.

Investigators followed up on her statements in September 1999, when Catherine Deely reached out to Brooks Brown. Deely had set up a site to support Columbine victims, including Brown. Brenda Parker had connected with her via her website and started communicating with her. Parker forwarded an email to her that she supposedly sent to an organization called We Are Guns. In it, she was trying to purchase a TEC-9 and Catherine grew concerned.

When investigators re-interviewed Parker, she claimed she had been keeping in touch with Judy Brown, Brooks' mother, and that she went to see the Blair Witch Project with Brooks approximately two weeks prior to the interview with the investigators. She also told authorities she spent a lot of time on the Internet in chat rooms and on bulletin boards/forums. She said she met Deely two months ago and that Deely was from Boston (Deely was actually from Brighton). Parker said Deely used to have a website devoted to Eric Harris and Dylan Klebold called "A Memorial: Tears for Eric and Dylan". Authorities then asked her if she had ever told anyone on the Internet that she was involved in the shooting or had any prior knowledge about it. She denied doing so, at which point they asked her if she knew who VODKAREB and BOSTNBYTCH were. She told them that VODKAREB was her online screenname and that BOSTNBYTCH was Deely.

At that time, investigators showed her a post made by user VODKAREB to a bulletin board that read:

"Ok well I see that I can't trust ANYONE in this club so I took my pics and saying I am outa here!

P.S. Whoever copied the pics like I said not to, I will find out who you are and you better watch your back! OH GAWD why didn't I just go along with the plan? I could be with them right now BUT NO I WAS CHICKEN SHIT and now I have to be stuck here all by myself with pathetic little STUPIDHEADS! Well not no more! I guess I will do what I should've done on 4-20 Boom! No more pain!"

After reading it, Parker said she remembered writing the first part of it but that someone must have added that last part. But when you compare this with her verified writing, it has the same emphasis and capitalization habits. Investigators gave her a full copy of a 16-page log of a chat session between her and Deely. In it she told Deely that she was supposed to be involved in the shooting, but circumstances interfered, and she backed out. She supplied a very detailed account of how things were supposed to go if she were involved, including how Harris was supposed to pick her up at a bus stop and how they would escape to her house in the mountains. She told Deely she was Harris' girlfriend and at one point pretended to be possessed by the ghost of Dylan, which scared Deely, who kept telling Parker to go to bed and to seek professional help.

Parker took 20 minutes to read the log, after which she said that she did have that conversation with Deely but that she was describing a dream she had. The reporting agent read several portions of the log aloud and pointed out how it didn't sound like a dream but a conversation between two people. After lengthy discussion, Parker finally admitted she had been lying to Deely about everything. She had no prior knowledge of the shooting and had no intention of harming herself or others. She told investigators that she had "no life" and "spent way too much time on the Internet".

There were other people who claimed to have known one or both of the gunmen or somehow been involved. The earliest on record identified himself as "Mike Smith" to reporters on scene during the week of the shooting. He told them he was a point guard for Columbine's basketball team.

Smith gave detailed accounts of how school officials ignored hostility between the Trench Coat Mafia and the jocks who called them "gays" and "inbreeds". The story ran in *USA Today* and the *Philadelphia Inquirer*, later picked up by *Rivera Live* and the *Drudge Report*. But the real point guard for Columbine, the son of a Rocky Mountain News reporter, came forward to say there was no Mike Smith on the team. When reporters checked the facts, they discovered there was no Mike Smith enrolled at Columbine High. The media outlets soon posted retractions.

(THERE WAS NO) GAY ALAMO

The rumor of the shooters being gay was started by a couple of upset teens who were interviewed following the shooting. They claimed amongst other things that the shooters were gay. One also claimed the shooters were Satanists and into witchcraft. The gay rumor was spread on BBS (bulletin board systems) by people who weren't even in the same state.

One of the earliest was the hoax email about a "Gay Alamo". The original post was a "copied" email posted to alt.truecrime that said the shooting was orchestrated by a bunch of gay bikers who were making it their "gay Alamo". The email said more gay bikers were on their way, but none ever materialized for obvious reasons. But some people latched onto the idea of the gunmen being gay. Two young men in love who were picked on for daring to be different finally had enough and lashed out at their homophobic tormentors. What could be more tragic? Though not supported by facts, the notion carried over into forum posts and fictional films inspired by the shooting.

In today's world of technological oversaturation, AI and unending rabbit holes, you can find whatever you look for out there. The important thing is to seek the truth and always research things for yourself.

KLEBOLD WAS GAY RUMOR (MIKE CONNORS)

Mike Connors was a freelance journalist and part-time producer of public information shows. On September 7, 1999, he contacted CBI agent Robert Brown, an acquaintance of his who was on the Columbine High shooting case. Connors wanted a favor from him, but Brown was unable to help him. During the conversation, Connors told Brown that he had been chatting with Dylan Klebold before April 20, 1999, on the internet and on the telephone.

SETTING THE RECORD STRAIGHT

Brown followed up on the report on November 16, 1999, speaking to Connors on the phone. Connors claimed he couldn't remember exactly when he spoke to Klebold, but that the conversations took place on a Saturday approximately 4 weeks before the shooting. Connors claimed he was in a Denver chatroom looking at user profiles when he came across a disturbing one that belonged to Dylan Klebold. The profile said Klebold was a student at Columbine High School, he hated jocks and was "either anti-religion or anti-Christian", Connors couldn't remember which. The personal quote said Klebold wanted to kill students at high school.

The responsible thing to do would have been to alert authorities or the hosting service, but Connors told Brown he sent Klebold a personal message, then chatted with him via private message. He said he told Klebold he was a reporter who covered the OKC bombing, then asked Klebold why he wanted to kill people at his high school. According to Connors, Klebold told him that ¾ of the students deserved to die. When Connors asked why, Klebold supposedly said the students picked on him, were mean and judgmental. Connors then told Brown he tried to explain to Klebold how the OKC bombing affected the victims, their families, and how it ruined lives.

Connors said Klebold mentioned Eric Harris by name and told Connors that he and Harris were lovers. Connors told Brown he believed that Klebold was gay and was hitting on him., and that Klebold sent him photographs of himself and Harris via the Internet. He said he gave Klebold his home phone number. Connors claimed Klebold called him the next day; his caller ID said it was Dylan Klebold. Connors told Brown that the phone call lasted about 30 minutes, that Klebold talked "a lot" about his relationship with Harris and described himself as bisexual.

To be clear, the encounter Connors presented was that he gave a troubled 17-year-old boy who was "hitting on him" his personal phone number, so said minor could call and tell him – a 40-something-year-old strange man on the Internet – about his sex life. Klebold, who bottled everything up, had no personal cell phone, and wasn't terribly active on the Internet beyond playing video games with friends.

Supposedly Klebold asked Connors if he was Christian, to which Connors said "yes". He said Klebold "went off" on him, telling him that he was stupid for being a Christian and that the Christians in Klebold's school had been mean to him. Connors said the teen told him that he admired Hitler. Then he claimed Klebold wanted to meet him in person but Connors "decided against it". He said Klebold sent him a couple of messages about wanting to meet, but Connors didn't respond.

This report is part of what fuels the theory that the shooters were gay. However, during investigation, Connors was unable to produce any photographs or chat logs. When authorities looked at his phone records, there was nothing to support his claim that he'd spoken with Klebold. There was no evidence to back up Connors' strange story of being hit on by a homicidal minor, something he didn't tell anyone about until six months after the shooting – and then only as part of a casual conversation while he was fishing for information about the shooting. Despite lack of proof, this misinformation has made it into books about the shooting and spread as fact on the Internet.

That's the root of most of the confusion about the event: So many fake stories have been told by "trusted sources" without any due diligence on the part of the listeners. Without question some of these bogus stories have been passed on in books, news articles, and films audiences trust to tell them the truth.

As the Greek tragedian Euripedes said: "Question everything."

AFTERMATH

The day after the shooting, the Columbine area was still reeling from the attack. By then news had spread outside of Colorado, largely due to the rapid transmission of information online. People flooded in from all over to offer support, leave items at the memorials in Clement Park and the parking lot of the school, and to get a first-hand glimpse of what was happening.

Coffee shops and cafes were crowded with onlookers and reporters though no one apart from officials could get close to the school. Even the families of the deceased were not allowed to approach the area. This was particularly painful for the Rohrboughs, who had seen their son's body on the news the next morning and knew it was him. They were not allowed onto the school grounds to retrieve him or even be near him. Officials told them and other families that the bodies of their loved ones were boobytrapped and couldn't be moved from the property. The bodies remained where they lay until the following evening.

There were two sites at Clement Park where makeshift memorials appeared. One area was at the north boundary of the school grounds, from the staff parking lot on the east side of the building west to the baseball fields. At the northeast corner of the park was a lot where students without parking permits would park their cars during school hours. Rachel Scott and John Tomlin's vehicles were both soon covered in flowers and notes from grieving friends and family. Large portions of the park were completely hidden under candles and posterboard cards signed by mourners. Teddy bears and ribbons were added to the heaps. Athletic jackets and t-shirts marked up with messages of sympathy, rosaries and pinwheels, windchimes, bagged letters and more piled up more than two feet deep in some areas. Balloons fluttered in the wind.

Churches brought out hot cocoa for the masses that showed up. The Salvation Army established free food service for first responders on the scene. Traffic leading to Clement Park was backed up for miles, clear to the Rocky Mountains. Parking was almost impossible to find as the small lots weren't made to accommodate so many visitors. The sheer number of people who went to the memorial areas soon reduced the park's grass to mud. Everywhere surrounding the school, from Clement Park to the local coffee shop, the topic of discussion was the Columbine shooting.

Meanwhile, families of children who were still missing anxiously kept watch on the news and called the hospitals with fading hope that their child was one of the ones who were in surgery and unidentified at the time. The dead were not removed from the building until the bomb squads and forensic teams completely secured the area around 2:30 p.m. on April 21st. It wouldn't be until 5 p.m. that the identities of the dead were known, and families were contacted. By then, some of them had already heard from the news that their loved one was dead. Lauren Townsend's family was among those who got the dreadful information that way. Her mother, Dawn Anna, was contacted later that day by officials but by then the damage was already done.

ZANIS CROSSES

On April 27th, a carpenter from Chicago, Illinois named Greg Zanis responded to a request from victim Brian Anderson to make memorial crosses to honor the families of the victims. Zanis worked tirelessly to construct 15 crosses, one for each person who died. He transported the crosses across the country to place atop Rebel Hill in the park. Visitors to the memorial made the long trek up to hill to view and write messages on the crosses. Intermittent rain washed away all but the strongest ink, but the writing was quickly replaced by more. Heaps of flowers and letters two feet deep piled up around the crosses, an outpouring of compassion from people who were touched by what happened.

AFTERMATH

The crosses Zanis made for the shooters quickly became the subject of contention, with people leaving angry and condemning statements on them. The crosses were eventually removed, torn down by Brian Rohrbough, father of victim Danny Rohrbough, one of the first to die at Columbine. Rohrbough was assisted by his father Claude, and Danny's stepfather, Rich Petrone. The family had asked the police to relocate the crosses, but no action was taken. So, they acted themselves.

Zanis felt that the crosses were there to comfort the parents of those who died, and in his opinion the Klebolds and Harrises deserved comfort because they too had lost children. However, most bystanders who had an opinion on the matter sided with Rohrbough's family. Brian Rohrbough strongly felt that the people who murdered his child should not have a memorial right next to that of his son. In the end, Harris and Klebold's crosses were removed from the display for good, though Zanis did display them elsewhere for a time.

NRA CONVENTION

Among those visiting the Denver area in the wake of the shooting were attendees of the National Rifle Association (NRA) annual convention. The convention had been planned for over a year and moving or canceling a gathering of that size came with a multitude of demographic, financial, and PR issues that were deemed insurmountable. In 2021, the NPR news agency discovered that the NRA considered canceling the annual convention. In a private conference call held the day after the shooting, officials of the organization discussed strategy. They initially considered a more sympathetic stance and even discussed donating funds to the victims. They questioned the propriety of having an event that featured comedians and "kids fondling firearms" where the media could see. Though they were concerned with appearances and the event was insured, the group ultimately decided to go through with a scaled-down version of the convention.

NRA advertising Marion hammer said: *"Screw the insurance. The message that it will send is that even the NRA was brought to its knees, and the media will have a field day with it."*

The event, scaled back from three days to one, opened its doors on May 1, 1999. Roughly 3,000 attendees showed up. So did around 8,000 protesters, including Tom Mauser, the father of victim Daniel Mauser. He carried a sign that read: *"Don't let my son's death be in vain."*

The protest prompted NRA President Charlton Heston to give a defiant speech at the event wherein he told roughly 2,500 cheering supporters that the NRA was not to blame for what happened at Columbine.

Heston said: *"We cannot, we must not let tragedy lay waste to the most rare, hard-won right in history."*

The nation was split in the days after the shooting into two camps: One that lobbied for stronger gun control laws and those who opposed stricter measures. And while that was certainly a factor in the protest, the main issue wasn't gun control. It was with the inappropriateness of holding a gun convention right after the world's worst school shooting on record in the city where it happened.

BACK TO SCHOOL

For the final three weeks of school, Columbine students resumed their classes at nearby Chatfield High School. Starting May 3, 1999, Chatfield students attended classes during the morning while Columbine students took over in the afternoon until 6 p.m. They continued to attend the school until May 27th. Parents stood ready on the first day, handing out pamphlets on how to handle the media, which was a continuous and often unwanted presence.

While some of the kids were happy to resume school and some even wanted to return to Columbine High, many remained uneasy about attending school anywhere. Some felt they should have waited longer or suspended classes entirely. Some didn't feel safe anywhere. There was a noticeable difference in attitudes between those who had gotten out quickly and easily and those who were closer to the shooting or had been trapped in the school longer. The individuals who escaped harm and were out of the line of fire soonest approached the recovery phase with high spirits, cheering and a strong sense of prevailing in the face of hardship. Those who were trapped in the science room with Coach Dave Sanders as he was bleeding out and those who were hiding in the cafeteria were more withdrawn and understandably traumatized.

    Parents worried, with just cause, that there might be another shooting as there were a shocking number of people who sympathized with Harris and Klebold. Websites and forums blew up over the justification of their murder spree. The sheriff's office was inundated with threats and leads they had to follow up on, slowing down and confusing the investigation. Faith in the system was shaken.

    The process for students to retrieve their belongings from Columbine's campus was difficult and, in many cases, added more trauma as they had to describe what they had with them from memory and later were sent into the school to claim their things before the school was cleaned up or repaired. There were questions as to whether the bomb sweeps were thorough enough to allow students on the school grounds.

    For seniors, the return to the school was especially painful. They were only allowed in to retrieve their belongings which had been left of the stage of the auditorium. They weren't allowed to look around or go anywhere else in the school even though for many it would be the last time they saw the place. As the graduating class, they were deprived of the typical things the senior class would experience in their last two weeks of school. They couldn't say proper goodbyes to the campus or their younger friends. They were unable to attend "take back the school" rallies the next school year and were cut off from a large portion of the community support other students received in the years that followed. The class was largely forgotten, left to migrate to their adult lives still disoriented and traumatized. Some tried to jump right into college only to struggle with being in a classroom or library. Seeking employment was equally difficult for individuals struggling with PTSD some of them weren't even aware they had until a panic attack shut them down.

The Jefferson County School District struggled financially in the wake of the shootings. In addition to the short-term adjustments which they had to make to accommodate students in those last weeks, it was calculated they would need $50 million dollars over the next three years to cover the costs associated with the shooting. Coupled with the cost of the repairs Columbine High needed this total included strengthening security at 143 schools in the district and counseling for nearly 100,000 students and staff members. Insurance would cover some of the cost, it would not cover everything. This was during a time when the district had been planning to cut back on spending. They originally had a conference scheduled for April 20th to announce cuts in transportation, staff, and athletics. The conference was canceled but the issues precipitating it were still there.

To help with the enormous cost, Colorado Governor Bill Owens authorized a $1 million disaster relief fund for Arapahoe County, $500,000 of which went to Columbine specifically. President Bill Clinton pledged an additionally $1.5 million in federal disaster relief funding.

On the evening of April 20th, President Clinton addressed the nation with a touching speech. He cautioned people not to rush to judgment and to focus on directing love and support to the people of the Columbine community. This was reinforced by his closing statement:

"To the families who have lost their loved ones, to the parents who have lost their beloved children, to the wounded children and their families, to people of the community of Littleton, I can only say tonight that the prayers of the American people are with you."

AFTERMATH

On May 20th, Clinton and his wife, First Lady Hillary, went to Colorado. President Clinton strongly felt he needed to be there in person. He met with the families of the victims at the Light of the World Catholic Church in Littleton, talking with them individually rather than from a podium. He spoke with each of the families and heard their stories about their loved ones, injured and deceased. He visited with Frank DeAngelis and shared tears with the people he spoke with. He ended up being late to his speech at Dakota Ridge High School where Columbine's class of 1999 was graduating because he felt that he was needed more at the church.

Clinton remained involved in the healing process of Columbine over the years. His family contributed personal funds to secure the Columbine Memorial, and he attended the groundbreaking in 2006. As of 2024, he continues to keep in touch with Frank DeAngelis. During the 20th anniversary he was quoted about the shooting:

"How do you go on without letting it go? If you don't let it go, can you go on? If you go on, do you let it go and forget something really important?"

It was Clinton's opinion that the Columbine community had done a good job of finding that balance. It's something they continue to strive for 25 years after the fact.

LAWSUITS

In the years since the shooting, several of the Columbine families requested and even sued for the public release of the Basement Tapes so that the mentality of the shooters could be analyzed. In 2001, after *Westword* and the *Rocky Mountain News* both published portions of Eric Harris' journal, the *Denver Post* sued to have the rest of the evidence that was taken from the homes of the shooters released to the public, including the Basement Tapes. The tapes were also demanded in suits against Solvay Pharmaceuticals and in lawsuits against the parents of the gunmen. Following those suits, in 2007 U.S. District Judge Lewis Babcock sealed the parents' depositions for 20 years.

The sealing of the depositions and the quiet destruction of the Basement Tapes in 2011 disturbed many, including Brian Rohrbough, who said the act only deepened his distrust of the agency particularly considering how former Sheriff John Stone and former Jefferson County District Attorney Dave Thomas deceived the families about what they knew.

In November of 2001, U.S. District Judge Lewis Babcock dismissed eight of the lawsuits pending against Jefferson County Sheriff's Office and the Jefferson County School District, stating they met the claim of government immunity. The only lawsuit allowed to proceed was one brought by the family of Coach Dave Sanders. The Sanders family contended that police gave "repeated false assurances that help would be there in 10 minutes" to people over the phone who were providing first aid to the fallen teacher. Judge Babcock also ruled that a portion of lawsuits from Jeanna Park's family and Valeen Schnurr's family could proceed. The suing families claimed deputies failed to provide medical care outside the school.

That December, Brad and Misty Bernall, the parents of victim Cassie Bernall, settled their lawsuit against the Harrises and Klebolds. The terms were kept confidential.

Several of the Columbine families also sued Jefferson County and various officials involved with the official response during the crisis. The wording of one concluded:

"Allegedly, Defendants portrayed the events at Columbine as a "hostage situation," despite there being no "genuine basis" for this designation either during or after the shootings, to conceal that it was a "high risk situation". To the contrary, according to Plaintiffs it was clear to Defendants that Harris and Klebold were engaging in "nothing other than the murdering and maiming of students and other human targets." Throughout Harris' and Klebold's rampage, they gave no indication that there were any conditions or circumstances, such

AFTERMATH

as meeting any demands, that could induce the pair to stop their violent attack."

Most of the lawsuits against the individual local officials were dismissed due to government immunity. The families of the victims settled their suits against the school district and Frank DeAngelis for $1 million. The Shoels, who had filed a $250 million suit, tried to back out of the settlement, claiming they agreed to it by mistake. The Supreme Court rejected the claim. The Sanders lawsuit was allowed to proceed and settled for $1.5 million. In 2001, roughly 30 of the Columbine families settled their suits against the Harrises and Klebolds for $2.8 million. Mark Taylor's suit against Solvay Pharmaceuticals ended in 2003. Though some sources say he settled for a $10,000 donation to the American Cancer Society, no money was paid in exchange for the dismissal. The courts ruled in favor of Solvay Pharmaceuticals.

In 2012, Dr. Janet Parker, DVM, filed a petition against the United States on behalf of Mark Taylor alleging that since 2009, Taylor was forced to undergo psychiatric treatment without consent. The petition was rejected for various reasons including the fact that the petitioner wasn't authorized to represent Taylor.

47

LASTING IMPACT

Over the years since the Columbine shooting there have been several copycat attacks—415 people killed and 907 wounded in school shootings as of the time of this writing, according to *ABC News*. Compare the 6 school shootings in 1999 to those of 2024 so far: A whopping 47. Many of the attacks were carried out by individuals who wanted to achieve the same notoriety that Harris and Klebold received initially. I stopped reporting other school shootings on the updates to *A Columbine Site* when I learned there were people on the Internet talking about how they felt getting a mention on my site as a shooter was a goal to achieve.

But while there have been more deadly school shootings since 1999, the perpetrators were never able to achieve the shock and awe that the Columbine shooting did, for several reasons. First, the Columbine shooters weren't trying to copy anyone. Harris spewed righteous indignation in his writing about how they had the idea before Michael Carneal and Kip Kinkel made headlines. Historically there have been many school shootings, but the terrorist approach the shooters took at Columbine was unprecedented. The fact that they did it together was also rare, with the Arkansas shooting involving Andrew Golden and Mitchell Johnson standing out as the only other tandem shooters.

In the public eye, the gunmen who were inspired by the Columbine tragedy looked exactly like what they were: Copycats. Whenever there is a school shooting, many refer to it as a "a Columbine attack" or "pulling a Columbine". People who hungered for attention saw it as an imitable way to get famous. But it didn't make them look edgy or tough. If anything, the masses found them even more despicable for wanting to copy an event that caused so much suffering to so many innocent people. These copycats have worked alone in isolated events. Klebold and Harris didn't kick start a revolution against a modern-day caste system. While they developed a cult following, the people who revere them are often mentally ill or too young to fully grasp the situation. Young people who relate to the shooters typically grow out of the fascination once they've experienced more life and recognize Harris and Klebold weren't representing the bullied underdog but were entitled narcissists who hated everyone.

On April 16th, 2019, an 18-year-old Florida woman, Sol Pais, made headlines when the Miami Beach Police Department received a tip that there was a "potential school shooter who is infatuated with Columbine shooter Eric Harris" who might be a danger to others. Officials investigated her online conduct and discovered Pais had contacted several Florida gun sellers. They learned she bought a one-way ticket from Miami to Denver on April 14th.

Shortly after arriving in Denver, she purchased a pump-action shotgun. Columbine was put into lockdown and classes dismissed early. Several other Denver schools also closed since no one knew where Pais was. Her body was found on the 17th near Mount Evans. Forensics revealed she killed herself on the 15th. School operations returned to normal after that.

In 2024, state lawmaker Tom Sullivan used this case as an argument for Colorado to institute a mandatory waiting period for gun purchases.

CRISIS RESPONSE

With the rise of mass shootings more safeguards have come as well. More schools have metal detectors, resource officers on site, barred fences, and locked classroom doors when class is in session. More places require visitor badges and student IDs. In 2001, the shocking attack on the World Trade Center instituted even more security changes in the United States, with TSA becoming a fixture. Over two decades later, passengers are still having to remove their shoes at airports and submit to body scans.

Police procedure has changed in many places as well, not just Littleton, but the world over. Within the USA, several states now have specific 'active shooter' procedures in place. Some have specific training programs their officers go through that specifically deal with shooters in schools and other public places. Internationally, security policies have changed as places such as Erfurt suffered their own tragic rampages.

One thing that's different in the USA is how those active shooters are handled. A basic call-respond-resolve procedure was in place until 1966, when the clocktower shooting at the University of Texas occurred. Officers weren't trained in how to handle an individual with massive firepower, nor did they have proper protective gear or weapons. After that, tactical structure was developed to protect officers from engaging in a firefight they weren't equipped to handle. Officers were to wait for the arrival of specially trained and armed personnel. This is the method officers at Columbine were forced to follow. This approach has drastically changed all over the world. Many police departments have special task forces who carry heavy weapons and are trained to close in on a shooter. In the United States, the International Association of Chiefs of Police (IACP) now vouches for this protocol:

"In active shooter situations where ongoing deadly force is reasonably likely to be employed by a suspect and delay in taking law enforcement action could result in injury or death, immediate action by officers at the scene is necessary when such actions are deemed reasonable to prevent further injuries or loss of life."

After initial assessment an officer on scene can then decide whether to intervene immediately or wait for backup. Contacting command is mandatory. A Rescue Task Force (RTF) will be assembled and sent in to assist and evacuate victims. Additionally, there is a push from the Department of Justice to refer to these events as "active killer" events rather than shooter, to acknowledge that terrorist events such as these don't always involve guns, such as when a person uses a vehicle to run down pedestrians outside a crowded night club.

Mass killings are still happening, but the active time of most of these events has shortened, generally lasting minutes compared to the hours Columbine dealt with. Officer training now prioritizes ending the violence as quickly as possible is the primary goal now, as it has been acknowledged that the shorter an incident is, the less lives are lost. Also, the IACP has noted that most shooting victims can be saved if the bleeding is stopped in a timely manner.

Sadly, there have been several major mass killings including school shootings since 1999. Sadder still, some have been more deadly than Columbine, including Virginia Tech, Sandy Hook and Parkland. The Parkland shooting was particularly hard for survivors of Columbine as the news footage that came out looked so very much like what happened on April 20, 1999. Several of the survivors reached out to Parkland students, to help them start the healing journey, forming a pen pal network to help Stoneman Douglas High School students process what happened and prepare for the road to recovery.

Amy Over, who was a Columbine senior in 1999, said to them: *"There are going to be really dark days in the years ahead, but you'll learn coping skills to help manage the pain. Be true to yourself."*

Every state reacts differently to this sort of tragedy. Some tighten gun laws; others make them looser. Schools are different as well. Most have drills and simple training in how to handle an active shooter situation. "Run, hide, fight" protocol teaches kids as young as kindergarten how to barricade doors and to throw things at an intruder to distract them. There are more security cameras on campuses and more security personnel. Classroom doors can be locked from the inside. Some operate on a security system that can lock all doors simultaneously in the event of a threat. Offices with windows have bullet-proof glass. Bars surround campuses. It's left many schools looking and feeling more like penal institutions than places of learning.

More crisis centers exist now to assist victims and their families. There are better protocols in place in most states where it comes to handling the aftermath of tragedy, whether it's a shooting or a natural disaster. Aid is easier to reach for many and there's a general sense of involvement that people have worldwide when it comes to assisting others during times of crisis.

Parents in general are more welcome in the classrooms of schools, both as volunteers and just to provide peace of mind. Many US schools now support "Safe2Tell" and similar programs that encourage students to tell adults when they see or hear others doing things that could be harmful. School resource officers have told me they've seen an uptick in reporting as students don't wish to be around people who could potentially hurt them or their school experience.

As new schools are built in Colorado and abroad, it is done with an eye to security, and the safety of those who will be there. Though a school will have multiple exits, there is usually only one or two ways to enter the campus, and those entrances are monitored by security. In 2018, the Federal School Safety Commission examined how statutes and regulations have changed. Among them are the subjects of character development and culture of connectedness, cyberbullying, mental health and counseling, anonymous reporting, security, active shooter preparedness, and training of school personnel.

Something that has changed at Columbine and many other schools throughout the United States is that in addition to fire drills, the school now has lockdown drills and secure perimeter drills. The National Center for Education Statistics says that 96% of schools in the United States now has a written plan for active shooter situations. Regardless of the drill, the faculty at Columbine High is careful to announce in advance any drill they intend to have so that those who might be triggered can make plans to avoid the school that day. The drills themselves are vetted as well. Drills that are too realistic could have the risk of causing emotional and psychological harm in participants. In that same vein of logic, the school no longer shows war movies in class.

In the broader Columbine community, things have changed as well. In 2004, Colorado adopted a Safe2Tell anonymous reporting system that SRO Ebling said was very successful. Since its start nationwide, the Safe2Tell reporting system has had over 160,000 reports, according to the attorney general. Most of the reports revolve around suicide or bullying, though several have been threats against schools. As of 2019, all states in the U.S. have laws that address bullying and cyberbullying.

In Wheat Ridge, decommissioned Martensen Elementary School was repurposed into the Frank DeAngelis Community Safety Center in 2017 as a training ground for law enforcement, first responders, and educators nationwide so they can prepare for an active killer situation. They engage in tough conversations, discuss and test tactics, share experiences, failures, and successes they've had. In addition to active shooter protocol, the center also offers de-escalation training, threat assessment, suicide prevention, and women's self-defense. As of 2024, the center has trained over 16,500 individuals.

Jeff Pierson, the executive director of Safety and Security at Jefferson County Public Schools, oversees 160 security personnel for the district, some of whom are armed. Pierson is a highly decorated police officer with FEMA and RAID certification. Responsible for the SROs in Denver's schools, he places priority on training new staff in how to manage incidents and to take their responsibilities seriously. All new school principals are trained at the Frank DeAngelis Community Safety Center where they are given scenarios to work through. They focus on emergency prevention as well as response. Prevention is preferable to reaction. JeffCo also has an emergency management team, campus supervisors, and threat assessment teams. There was no shortage of security during my visit to Columbine on April 20th, 2024.

ZERO-TOLERANCE

Along with safe reporting, most schools in the United States adopted a "Zero Tolerance" policy. Ideally, this policy was instituted to establish rules and guidelines for students to follow that would reduce the risk of violence in schools. Failure to follow these rules would result in suspension or expulsion, and in rare cases legal action. Common subjects that these zero-tolerance policies address are threats, physical altercations, and possession/use of drugs or weapons. In addition to students, these policies typically extend to staff, parents, and visitors to the campus.

But while the intention behind the approach is sincere, studies have shown that Zero Tolerance isn't very effective. The policies do not deter unwanted behavior and generally make the school campus a more authoritarian and uncomfortable place to be for all. The addition of bars around many schools has only increased the penal institution impression. And while they may appear to make the campus more secure, often gates are left unlocked and even wedged open, so the effectiveness of the barrier is compromised. Bullying is still present in many schools, and the amount of violent and drug-related issues is on the rise. Moreover, the punitive zero-tolerance approach has been proven to engender mistrust in students toward adults and inhibit the formation of school bonds.

Studies show a better alternative to Zero-Tolerance is building connections between students, staff, and their school. Students who trust their teachers are more likely to behave well for them and do better in their academics. Character education and social learning programs not only encourage kids to talk and bond with one another, it helps many people learn how to get along with others. Targeted support for at-risk students, including cognitive behavioral training and intervention programs show strong evidence of working in schools that have instituted them. These types of programs engage students in daily or weekly exercises to build and practice social skills. They help these at-risk kids learn how to manage their emotions and promote bonding between students.

There are a lot of children growing up who haven't had proper socialization instruction. There are many reasons behind this deficit. Home-schooling has grown more popular in the past two decades but has had little to no supervision from the states, and home-schooling does not provide daily peer-to-peer socialization. During the pandemic, all the schools were put into online mode.

There are at least two grade levels of kids who started school at home and had to migrate to in-person study, facing social challenges previous generations did not. The drug problem in the United States has further complicated things, with a record number of children being born into low-income, single-parent households where adult supervision is inadequate. Kids who would flourish in a stable, socially connected environment aren't getting off on the right foot and are being thrust into classrooms where the pressure is on to conform to social rules they have never been exposed to. Education and communication are essential to tipping this balance. Systems that punish don't correct the fundamental issues where it comes to secure bonding and learning how to manage one's emotions and environmental stress.

IMPACT ON MEDIA

Another area where the shooting at Columbine has had a lasting impact is on the media. Dozens of books, plays, films, and songs have been written about or inspired by the event. Some of these contributions have been uplifting or insightful. Others have been repulsive.

At least two independent, amateur games were made about the shooting. A small studio briefly offered action figures based on the gunmen. Likewise, skins based on the shooters cropped up for games that were popular at the time and a shocking amount of fan fiction has turned up online.

There have been several films, both serious and mocking, that have fictionalized the events or been inspired to tell a romanticized version of what happened. Some take the viewpoint of a victim or survivor of this or a similar fictional school shooting. Some even take the viewpoint of the shooters. There have been countless television shows that used the hot-button topic to boost ratings and shake up their audiences. More than one has featured the school shooter as a sympathetic or misunderstood character. There have been plays and performative thought pieces and hundreds of books written about the shooting, some with glaring inaccuracies that authors refused to revise even after being contacted by families of the victims.

But the amount of positive creativity has outweighed the negative. Musical groups have created songs memorializing the victims and offering hope. Insightful plays and films have made waves in the industry. There has been a push to put the focus of news programs on the victims and the survivors rather than their attackers. Not just with Columbine but other crisis events in recent times. News outlets are more aware of the effects of the way a story is presented and there are journalists pushing for new guidelines to govern how stories are worded. They are leaning away from mentioning the names of perpetrators in article titles and focusing more on the effects of the event on the families and communities involved, rather than the motives and backgrounds of the perps themselves.

Over the years the media has adopted new methods about how they handle mass shootings and other tragic event reporting. In the USA, it is now standard policy to hold off releasing them names of deceased victims until the families have been notified. News outlets also understand the Internet better and no longer take everything posted to the Web as fact. More research is done, more questions asked, more proof is demanded. More media outlets are holding off reporting on details until they've confirmed the situation, which they tell their audience. In the case of the 2012 Aurora theater shooting, at least one news station announced that it would not be discussing further details about the shooter unless there was some major court decision that affected the development of the case.

Local news agencies in Colorado saw the damage their reports were causing and shifted gears from focusing on the shooters and the devastation to stories of survival and success. They tried harder to present factual information. Over the years, the message about public shooters in general has switched from "Look at what they did to that group!" to "How could they do this to us?"

In other nations such as Ireland, the focus of media reports is placed on the victims and what their loss has done to the families and the community. The perpetrator is a footnote, sometimes not even given a name. Interviews aim to share the feelings of the people who cared about the deceased and the history of the life that was lost, rather than the motives and background of their killer.

Before 1999, just about anything could be sold online via the fledgling website eBay, which started in 1995. There was very little regulation on what a seller could list. As such, there was a bloom in "murderabilia" on the site after the shooting at Columbine: items related to murders, the perpetrators, or other violent crimes. Everything from Columbine yearbooks to inappropriate artwork was being shilled. In 2001, eBay clamped down on the sale of all murderabilia. I was still able to sell CD backups of my website through the platform, but only because it was news, not a glorification of crime or the killers. The CDs were an archive of the site for researchers to use offline as a thank you gift to people who helped pay the hosting bills for aColumbineSite.com. The CD gift was discontinued when shipping costs got too expensive.

YouTube also eventually had to put in place stricter policies regarding what sort of videos could be uploaded regarding Columbine and other tragic events. While news clips are allowed, anything that focuses too much on the perpetrators of crimes is quickly flagged and removed from the site. For example, you can't upload one of the videos the shooters created before the massacre even though it might show only the commercial for bicycle wax.

Lasting impact from the tragedy at Columbine on social media can be seen in the multitude of conspiracy blogs and forums that feature fictionalized ideas of what the killers were like. Both are equally problematic in their own ways. The danger with that sort of thinking is it removes the reality of what happened and interjects self-insert notions of what the writers want to believe. Whether it's a conspiracy or a romanticization, both approaches put the focus on things that aren't real over the true tragic actions and consequences that came from that horrible day. It also downplays or eradicates the suffering that so many people went through.

There are people who go looking on the Internet for information who then find these websites and fall down rabbit holes without doing further research. They get locked into whatever narrative the sites are spinning and promote that story regardless of what's real. It's a difficult thing to argue with too once someone has decided that is their truth. Once a person has embraced an idea, it becomes their idea, and few people like to be told they're wrong about something they feel strongly about. What you look for in life you will find. Unfortunately, you can find anything on the World Wide Web if you seek it out.

Over time, the angle of news stories about the Columbine shooting have shifted to focus on how the survivors are doing and what the families of those who were killed have gone on to do. In many cases these are inspiring stories of overcoming tragedy. Dave Cullen addressed the failings of the media in his recent article on *The Guardian*. In it he acknowledged how reporting, including his own, skewed the narrative in ways that can't be erased but can be addressed going forward to help curb the idealization of fictionalized versions of Harris and Klebold.

Some of the recent stories about the survivors have taken a somber direction, sadly, such as the ongoing struggles of

LASTING IMPACT

Richard Castaldo and Mark Taylor. Austin Eubanks survived the shooting in the library and went on to become a public speaker, only to lose his life to overdose following the 20th anniversary of the Columbine shooting. Anne Marie Hochhalter lost her mother to suicide. Other suicides include Greg Barnes in 2000 and Joe Stair in 2007. Barnes, a varsity basketball player who saw Coach Dave Sanders get shot, died a month after the first anniversary of the tragedy at Columbine. Stair was a former Trench Coat Mafia member who came under scrutiny following the shooting. He died 5 weeks after the Virginia Tech shooting.

While Columbine's ripple effect has brought sorrow and the survivors were left with lasting scars both physical and psychological, many have found ways to move on. Many of the students have gone on to marry and have kids of their own. This has brought about a new viewpoint for many of them and they tend to be better connected with the school system their children belong to. As years have become decades, some of the survivors have followed the road of author, public speaker, or film maker and are involved in media coverage of Columbine. They can now shape the public perspective of the event they had to live through and through it make a difference for the future.

CHANGE AND LACK THEREOF

Though much has changed over the years, some things have not.

For Sue Petrone, the time capsule effect is real. She has seen the children of her friends and family grow up over the years. Her son Dan Rohrbough, one of the first victims killed, will always be 15. When she ran into a friend of Danny's who was now a grown man, she realized just how long it had been. Her son's birthday leads her to question what he would have been like and if he would have had kids of his own.

The same is true for Tom Mauser. His son Daniel, who died in the library, will always be 15 years old in his mind. Though his son should be 40 as of 2024, it doesn't feel to him as though it's been 25 years. He still lobbies for gun control in the United States and has seen very little change on that front. Tom still speaks publicly about his son and the shooting. He still gets choked up when he talks about losing his son. It's his hope that the nation will eventually adopt a "red flag" law that would allow safe reporting for everyone, much like Safe2Tell has done for schools. But he has seen some good come of things when the national bipartisan Safer Communities Act passed in 2022.

September 2023, President Joe Biden's administration created the White House Office of Gun Violence Prevention and implemented the largest expansion of the gun background check requirement since 1993. The expanded background check was created in part to address the loophole that allowed the Columbine shooters to acquire their guns.

Tom still wears Daniel's size 10.5 sneakers at special events, including to the 2024 public memorial service. It was held on the evening of April 19th at the First Baptist Church in Denver. The memorial was organized by Tom Mauser and a handful of supporters and advocates when they learned that there wasn't going to be an official public event for the 25th anniversary.

Thirteen empty chairs were stationed to remember the victims who were killed, lit by small candles. Mauser wore his son's tennis shoes—the ones Daniel was wearing the day he was killed. Mauser wears the shoes only for special occasions to preserve them. Coni Sanders, daughter of Coach Dave Sanders, was in attendance as well and spoke at the vigil at the First Baptist Church in Denver. She told the assembled crowd, some 150 people, that her father helped save hundreds of kids that day. Those kids grew up to have children of their own and those kids will eventually have kids of their own thanks to her father's sacrifice.

English teacher Kiki Leyba was at the vigil, wearing a gray and blue baseball jersey that had his name and the year he was hired on it—a shirt all of Columbine's staff have.

LASTING IMPACT

He was in a meeting with Principal DeAngelis on the morning of April 20, 1999. His contract as a temp was ending and Mr. De was getting ready to offer him a full-time position at the school. What should have been a happy meeting was interrupted with the principal's assistant burst into the room to tell them there were shots fired in the halls of Columbine. DeAngelis and Leyba sprang into action, clearing students from the halls as the shooters were coming toward the front office area.

Leyba said at the vigil that he never seriously considered leaving the school after the tragedy, though in June 1999, he experienced a serious setback while working with the Jefferson County Open Space Youth Work Program. It was his second year with the group repairing and building hiking trails with teens and college students in the Front Range Mountains. As they were heading back down the mountain, a storm hit. Though he had weathered many storms since he was a boy in Scouts, that one was particularly severe as was his reaction to it. He called for the group to take shelter as they were trained to, to protect themselves from lightning. While crouched down, a bolt struck the ground right behind him. The situation left Leyba frantic and in tears, but he stayed with his group who needed him.

Recovery has been a slow but steady process for Leyba, guided by therapy and outreach to schools and the support of his wife Kallie.

"Every year feels closer to what I once knew as normal. Life is a shoreline, a wet-dry line between normal and the awkward."

For Leyba, a part of normal is teaching. In 2003, Sean Graves, a victim of the shooting, returned to Columbine and spoke with Leyba's writing class. Graves was one of the first victims and was shot outside the cafeteria and nearly paralyzed. He shared his story with Leyba and his students. That moment was one of the most healing for him.

Nathan Hochhalter, another survivor, also spoke the memorial in 2024. He was a freshman trapped in a classroom at

Columbine during the shooting. His older sister Anne Marie was almost killed by the shooters outside and his mother Carla committed suicide in October 1999. Nate told the assembly at the memorial:

> *"I just want to use this moment to let everyone know that it's OK to ask for help. Whatever your situation is, whether either as a survivor 25 years later or someone struggling with any part of their life, these things come in waves, and they can hit you when you least expect it. You should all know that we're all here for you and that you're not alone."*

RACHEL'S CHALLENGE

Rachels' Challenge is a non-profit organization founded by the family of Rachel Scott. It focuses on community, healing, and positive attitude. In their own words, the organization addresses the roots of school violence, bullying, and self-harm. They promote connection and hope within school culture

Darrell Scott, Rachel's father, calls it a "for" club. They're not against bullying, they're for kindness. In her diary, Rachel wrote about wanting "to start a chain reaction" of kindness in the world. Rachel's Challenge brings people together by following Rachel's own example of enacting simple acts of kindness and compassion.

The Challenge strives to create change through forgiveness, hope, and social-emotional learning. The goal of the organization is to tackle the causes of school violence and self-harm with empathy and kindness. In her writings, Rachel called it a "chain reaction". The program has reached over 30 million students as of 2022, with roughly 150 suicides averted annually. The group offers programs for every school level, elementary to high school, and even offers keynote speeches.

When he started the non-religious organization, it was Scott's intent to honor his daughter for one year. To share her

LASTING IMPACT

story and let the world know who she was. Twenty-five years later, Rachel's Challenge is still active and going strong. Every year the group holds talks at schools where they challenge kids to join the "for club". It's Scott's wish to fight the increase in the negative influences out there with the positive.

You can find information in the Resources section at the back of this book on how to get involved with Rachel's Challenge.

THE COLUMBINE FAMILIES

I generally don't approach the Columbine families about the shooting. I've known for a long time how the constant press of curious onlookers has affected them, and I never wanted to be a part of that negative experience for them. Besides sending out notice of my intent to publish books to those with public contact information and socializing with individuals at memorials, I have largely left them alone. I have an open invitation on my site and in my books for anyone involved to share their stories, updates, or corrections. However, I don't want to hound anyone about an event many wish to put behind them. While I feel it's important to share the stories of the Columbine families, I won't do it at the cost of adding to the pain of those who survived it. No one should have to have their whole lives shaped by a single tragic event.

The group of people who survived the shooting is a large one, encompassing those who were at the school, their families, the first responders, the counselors and other response that followed, and the Columbine community which was turned upside down, forever altered due to the events of that tragic day. They have had 25 years to work through the impact it had on their lives. Each has dealt with it in their own way. For many, coming together to support each other through the hard times has been essential. From several families came one bigger Columbine family that still exists today. I was honored to meet several members on my trip to Colorado.

Spending time with the Columbine family was an uplifting and inspirational experience. They have come through the darkest of times and truly embodied the spirit of hope and renewal.

THE PEOPLE

This section has been included after careful consideration. While this book emphasizes the healing journey ahead, it would

COLUMBINE NOW

be remiss to discuss Columbine without paying tribute to those who were most affected by the event. The content in this section seeks to honor the positive traits of the people mentioned. It is a combination of known facts, lesser-known facts, and information that corrects some misconceptions. It is written with a focus on the inspiration that can be taken from the lives of the individuals.

While some of the people I've spoken with wish to leave Columbine behind, the majority want to see some good come from what they've been through. Focusing on that goal helps the healing process, as does seeing the positive change that goal inspires. Craig Scott, Beth Nimmo, Darrell Scott, Dawn Anna, Frank DeAngelis, Crystal Woodman, Kacey Ruegsegger, Tom Mauser, Linda Sanders, Misty Bernall, Brooks Brown, and Sue Klebold have all written books about their experience. Families of some of the survivors, including Patrick Ireland and Brian Anderson, have reached out to me to share their successes in life. Sean Graves, Diwata Perez, and Lance Kirklin have been involved in documentary retrospectives.

Over time, some of the stories that came out of that day have gotten conflated and rewritten, either to push someone's agenda or to bring in money. Some of the survivors have been tricked by people into saying things that have then been edited and revised to fit the story those individuals wanted to peddle. Worse, a few of the victims are in a compromised mental state where they will either agree to anything they're told from a source they think they can trust, or they simply can't communicate for themselves anymore.

Mark Taylor is one of those unfortunate individuals. After his long recovery, in 2006 he ghost-wrote a book that put a strong religious spin on his experience but was "not in a state to promote it" according to the publisher. Following an alleged public meltdown in a Borders bookstore in 2008, he was treated by Dr. William Deagle who turned out to be quite nefarious: The man was a known conspiracy theorist who would show up at high-profile tragic events such as the Oklahoma City bombing to offer his services to the families of victims. His medical license was suspended in 2004 because of the death of one three patients he overprescribed medication to. Since that time, Deagle was hit with at least one other wrongful death suit following the suspicious death of one of his patients.

Mark was hospitalized and put on strong drugs that zombified him to the point that he could no longer answer basic questions such as where he was living and who was caring for him, despite the fact he was sitting beside his mother whom he lived with. Donna Taylor, Mark's mother, later broke off contact with Deagle over concerns that he was overprescribing medication to her son and that the doctor was trying to control them. In 2007, the Colorado state board revoked Deagle's license to practice medicine regarding 6 more overprescribing cases. The Taylors' last verified known location as of this writing was in a homeless shelter where they were seeking to raise money for Mark's ongoing medical expenses.

Likewise, Richard Castaldo has had a rocky time trying to stabilize in life. Wheelchair bound, he has been homeless and too sick to care for himself. He has been taken advantage of by film makers such as Michael Moore and by authors who wanted to claim that he, too, told the shooters he believed in God. Each time he's been used to push someone else's agenda, it has been of no benefit to him and has clouded his memory of events to the point where he can't even be sure of what happened to him.

Fortunately, there are more people who have managed to take their situation and cultivate some positive from it. Individuals such as Crystal Woodman and Kacey Ruegsegger, both of whom were in the library during the shooting, went on to get married and write inspirational books about their experiences. The staff members and counselors I've spoken with are all still gainfully employed and actively making a difference in community programs and at schools including Columbine. Patrick Ireland, the boy in the window, went on to become a successful real estate agent. Sean Graves, who was gunned down outside the cafeteria and watched his friends die, is happily married with children.

COLUMBINE NOW

Despite being in a wheelchair, Anne Marie Hochhalter went on to graduate from college and to become a manager at Bath and Body Works. She and Sue Townsend, Lauren Townsend's mother-in-law, became friends when Townsend volunteered to drive Hochhalter to physical therapy. The lingering connections from the shooting find ways to surface even years later. In an interview with US News during the 10th anniversary of the shooting, Hochhalter related how she had been at a grocery store and the cashier asked her why she was in a wheelchair. When she told the clerk she had been shot at Columbine, a man from the line behind her came forward to tell her he was part of the SWAT team and was sorry they couldn't get to her sooner. She told him that she didn't blame him and looks at the exchange as one of the greatest moments of her life.

Andrew Robinson, who was a senior in 1999 and in the Tech Lab when the shooting occurred, later went on to become a film writer, director, and producer. A friend of Rachel Scott's, his first film *April Showers* shows how a survivor of a school shooting copes with loss. The indie film *Reunion: 13 Worth Remembering* imagines what life would have been like for the victims had they not been killed.

In October 2000, the Mauser family adopted a baby as part of their process of healing from the loss of their son Daniel. Tom Mauser, who became a vocal activist in the wake of his son's death and wore his son's shoes to rallies and other important events, wrote about the adoption process on their memorial website. Their daughter Christine got to pick her name: Madeline. Madeline later graduated from Heritage High in Denver. Tom still campaigns for stricter gun laws in the United States.

Several of the survivors and their families went on to become public speakers who have given presentations at hundreds of schools and other venues. Sue Klebold, for instance, became an active public speaker who was featured on TED Talks and several television shows. She seeks to make a difference, to ease public opinion, and to help prevent tragedy in the future.

Heather Martin, a senior who hid in an office during the shooting at Columbine, co-founded The Rebels Project in 2012 following the Aurora theater shooting to help survivors of any mass shooting. She went on to become an English teacher at Aurora Central High School.

Frank DeAngelis started a charity, the Frank DeAngelis Academic Foundation which supports the academic needs of Columbine that aren't met by funds from the school district. The foundation also contributes to the annual 5K fun run. Mr. De is also a board member of the Columbine Memorial Foundation, which was formed after the official memorial was constructed. The group facilitates repairs and maintenance of the memorial. Other board members include or have included Bob Curnow, father of victim Steven Curnow, and Lee Andres, a choir teacher who helped evacuate students from the school.

The people who make up the Columbine Family don't all see eye to eye. They don't all agree on how best to proceed. But everyone I've interacted with has been incredibly strong and motivated to see positive change come into the world to make up for everything they've been through. Taking tragedy and turning it to triumph is an amazing ideal any person can strive for.

COLUMBINE NOW

THOSE WHO DIED

The information below is public knowledge, sourced from interviews with the families and from books they wrote. It's a snapshot of who they were, included to provide a better understanding of what they were like and what mattered to them. Some entries are longer because their families have shared more about them over the years. Even the lives that were lost have come to represent hope and healing in their own unique ways.

Cassie Bernall

Born November 6, 1981, Cassie was a 17-year-old junior at Columbine. She grew up in an evangelical Christian home with parents Misty and Brad Bernall and her younger brother Chris. She loved to go rock climbing in Breckinridge, swimming, and riding bikes with her dad. Her favorite movie was *Braveheart*.

    Cassie, like many her age, recently struggled on her teenage road to self-discovery. She rebelled against her upbringing, tried out the Goth scene and even dabbled in witchcraft. She experimented with drugs and alcohol. When she was 15, her mother found notes Cassie and her best friend had been writing to each other that spoke of killing their parents and teachers. The Bernalls transferred their daughter to a private school. Cut off from her friends and angry with her parents, Cassie spiraled into depression, writing poems about suicide.

    Eventually, Cassie made new friends. She found support in the youth programs at the church her family attended. She found her way back to religion after attending a religious summer camp in 1997, where she became a born-again Christian. That fall, her parents let her transfer out of private school and into Columbine High where she did well in academics. She got into Shakespeare and photography. Life was getting better for her.

    Then came that fateful day in the library.

For a long time after the shootings, it was believed she was the girl in the library who was asked at gunpoint: *"Do you believe in God?"*. It was thought that he shot her because she said *"Yes"*. The idea was inspiring to many, including her mother, who wrote a book about her daughter titled *She Said Yes: The Unlikely Martyrdom of Cassie Bernall* (published Sept. 1, 1999).

Eventually it came out that the conversation occurred between the gunman and injured victim Valeen Schnurr. Emily Wyant, who was hiding beside Cassie, told the FBI and *Rocky Mountain News* the real story but they withheld the information from the public so as not to make things difficult for the Bernalls. On September 30, 1999, *Salon.com* reporter Dave Cullen exposed what really happened but by then it didn't matter. The exchange might not have been real, people latched onto the ideal of standing strong in the face of adversity. Though she didn't say anything to the gunmen, the story of the girl who said "yes" still inspires people all over the world. Her family prefers to think of her as that girl.

Cassie was laid to rest in Golden Cemetery in Golden, Colorado.

Steve Curnow

Born August 26, 1984, Steve was a 14-year-old freshman at Columbine. He was the youngest victim. He dreamed of being a Navy top gun pilot. Though his parents were divorced he was very close with both his mom Susan (Susie) and his father Robert (Bob).

Steve loved soccer and started playing at age 5 with the YMCA. He later played for Club Columbine. When he discovered his soccer skills weren't strong enough to make the team at Columbine High, he continued to play on the team his dad coached, the Colorado Rush Soccer Association. His father encouraged him to explore being a referee and helped him train for the position. By being a part-time referee Steve learned the game better and earned some money, too. Steve liked green because it was the color of the field. His favorite classes were Spanish, technology, and gym because he got to play sports. He dreamed of becoming an aviator after discovering the joy of flight during a family vacation to England.

He was a huge fan of the *Star Wars* series. He watched the films so many times, he could recite the dialogue along with the actors. Science fiction fans nationwide put together a "Go to Star Wars" day in his honor when *Star Wars I: the Phantom Menace* premiered in theaters on May 19th, 1999. He had been anxiously awaiting its release.

Steve was buried in Fort Logan National Cemetery in Denver, Colorado.

Corey DePooter

Born March 3, 1982, Corey DePooter was a 17-year-old former wrestler who loved to hike, golf, hunt, and fish. He enjoyed wrestling, golf and in-line skating, but fishing was his passion. He had recently taken a maintenance job at a golf club to save up to buy a fishing boat with a friend. Someone Corey used to fish with said: *"It was the times we didn't do well that his personality really shined."* Another friend said of him: *"When you're going fishing or camping, I know he's going to be there, watching and making sure you're doing everything right."*

A junior at Columbine at the time of the shootings, Corey is described as an all-American kid who put schoolwork above everything else: He had his wisdom teeth removed that year and was upset that the procedure forced him to miss school. His sister Jena was a freshman at the high school when he died. He taught her how to fly fish and they used to hike together along the mountain stream at their family's favorite camping spot near Buena Vista. To cope with her loss, Jena said she liked to imagine her brother was doing something he loved.

Corey's best friend Austin Eubanks was with him in the library when he was killed. Austin later said about Corey: *"People said he was the kind of guy people like to be around. I know I sure did. Corey was always able to pick our spirits up in a gloomy situation."*

The day he died Corey was supposed to go to the bank with his father Neal to get a loan for a used Mustang. His condition for getting the car was he had to keep his grades up. Neal described his son as an all-American boy.

The DePooters received thousands of cards and letters from around the world after Corey's death. They read every one, finding they helped the healing process even though they couldn't personally respond to them all. They were especially touched by the encouraging letters they received from children. During the weeks that followed the shooting, the family grew close to the other victims' families, meeting weekly and gathering monthly for potluck meals. By engaging in community projects together and leaning on each other when the days were worst, they found true friendship.

Corey's funeral was held at Trinity Christian Center. Soon after his death his grandmother, Fern Hamilton, contacted the Marine Corps about holding some sort of ceremony for Corey because he'd always wanted to become a Marine. On May 3, 2000, Corey was granted that dream during a ceremony at his gravesite in Chapel Hill Memorial Gardens in Littleton, Colorado, where he was made an honorary Marine.

Kelly Fleming

Kelly was born January 6, 1983. The 16-year-old and her family moved to Littleton from Phoenix, Arizona 18 months before the shooting. Her father Don said they scoured the area looking for a good neighborhood where their daughters would be safe.

A shy and creative girl who loved Halloween, Kelly was an aspiring songwriter and author who wrote many poems and

COLUMBINE NOW

short stories based on her life experiences. She had been writing an autobiography on her home computer: She started the story with the moment her mother's water broke and had gotten as far as her fifth year. She regularly went to Columbine's library to write. Her stories often had happy endings.

Kelly was learning to drive and wanted to get a job at a day care center and save enough money to buy a Mustang or a Corvette. She longed to be able to drive so she could return to Phoenix for a visit or go on road trips. She loved to read, especially books about vampires. One day she hoped to be a published author. She entered many writing contests.

Her math first semester math teacher at Columbine in 1999, Jud Blatchford, said about Kelly: *"She was one of the kindest students I've ever had. She was really shy. She would never read them [her stories] to me."* She would hand him the paper and let Blatchford read it himself. She often wrote about herself and the struggles she faced. Her stories and poems often had happy endings. Blatchford served as one of the pallbearers at her funeral.

Her mother, Dee, remembered Kelly coming home from school two months before the shooting, saying: *"I'm not shy anymore."*

Kelly's funeral was held at the same time as Daniel Mauser's at the St. Frances Cabrini Catholic Church. She was buried with two teddy bears in her arms. Her grave is located at Mount Olivet Cemetery in Wheat Ridge, Colorado. In the days that followed, neighbors of the Flemings brought them pizza, bagels, flowers, and food trays. They shoveled snow from the Flemings' sidewalk out front and tied a bow around the tree in their yard. Kelly's father said he and his family felt as safe as ever in the community.

Matt Kechter

Born February 19, 1983, Matt was a sturdy 210-pound sophomore. The 16-year-old played on both the offensive and defensive lines of the football team. He's remembered for his ready laugh. He was a weightlifter and an 'A' student, always getting good grades in school.

"When I heard he was one of the ones from the library, it only made sense," said sophomore basketball player and close friend Greg Barnes. *"He was always in the library studying. He always put academics first,"* Greg said of Matt. *"He had straight A's but he would never brag about it. I kinda looked up to him because of it. He was never in a bad mood, he was consistently happy."*

Other friends described Matt as a sweet, shy guy. Neighbors remembered him as a straight-A student who had "tons of friends" and frequently played basketball in the family driveway with his younger brother Adam.

"He was a wonderful role model for his little brother," his parents wrote in a statement that was read at his funeral at St. Frances Cabrini Catholic Church on April 27. *"Their brotherhood had just recently developed into a bonding friendship ... In Matt's heart, there was always enough room for everyone to be victorious."*

Days after the shooting, his mother Ann slept in his dirty clothes just to feel close to her son. In 2001, Ann and Joe fostered an 8-year-old girl. Two years later, they adopted her.

"We were not trying to replace Matt, but we have a lot of love to give," Ann said. *"We feel more complete as a family."*

The University of Colorado where Matt had planned to attend sent his brother Adam one of their jerseys bearing Matt's name and the jersey number he wore, 70, as part of Columbine's football team. The Columbine High School football team all wore ribbons bearing his old jersey number and were asked to dedicate the next season to Matt's memory at his funeral service.

COLUMBINE NOW

Matt was buried in Mount Olivet Cemetery in Wheat Ridge, Colorado. In September of 1999, Matt Kechter was posthumously accepted into the National Honor Society.

Daniel Mauser

Born June 25, 1983, Daniel was a 15-year-old sophomore who excelled in math and science. He received straight 'A's in his classes for the last two grading periods and posthumously won the "Stretch for Excellence" award for being named the top biology student of the Sophomore class at Columbine High School. Dan was shy but didn't let that stop him from joining the debate team. And though he wasn't a natural athlete, he joined the cross-country team. He liked to ski and camp. He had recently returned from a two-week trip to Paris with the French club. Daniel was also posthumously accepted for membership into the National Honor Society in September of 1999. He had applied for membership weeks before the shootings.

Daniel is described by his family as a shy, gentle soul; lovable and loving. His dad, Tom Mauser, remembered his son as a smart young man who wasn't afraid of challenges and who wasn't ashamed to hug his parents. He was close friends with his sister Christine. Dan liked pepperoni pizza, playing video and computer games, and watching shows like *The Simpsons* and *X-Files*. Daniel was fond of trivia and knowledge games, as well as swimming and hiking. His father had hoped that in the summer of 1999 to take Dan on his first 14,000 mountain hike.

Dan volunteered at the Swedish Hospital. He would have been Confirmed at St. Frances Cabrini Church two weeks after the date of his death. His class put a plaque in the teen program room in Daniel's honor. Dan was hoping to get his driver's license in 2000. He was concerned with gun safety in America – just two weeks before he was killed Daniel had asked his father if he knew that there were loopholes in the Brady Bill. Tom Mauser was motivated by what he interpreted as a sign of action: His son was shot with a gun that was purchased through one of the very loopholes Dan had pointed out. Tom is now an active protester of the NRA and continues to campaign for stricter gun laws.

Dan's funeral was held jointly with Kelly Fleming's at St. Frances Cabrini Catholic Church. He was buried in Mount Olivet Cemetery in Wheat Ridge, Colorado.

Not long after the shootings, Daniel's family along with several other families of the shooting victims learned that the school district was planning to reopen the library where Dan and the others died. The plan was to make cosmetic changes such as removing the carpet, repainting, replacing bullet-riddled shelves. Upset by the notion, the Mausers along with several other parents and volunteers founded HOPE (Healing of People Everywhere) and together they convinced the district to tear out the old library and replace it.

Daniel Rohrbough

Daniel was born March 2, 1984. The quiet 15-year-old enjoyed electronics and computer games. He was looking forward to getting his driver's permit soon. Friends remembered Danny as a fun, zany guy who wore shorts in winter. He helped in his father's stereo business, Excalibur Sound Systems, every day after school and during the summer he worked on his grandfather's farm in Kansas harvesting wheat, as he had done since he was three. He used the money he earned to buy Christmas presents for his family.

His parents were divorced, but they made a pact to make raising Danny their number one priority. His mother married Rich Petrone, whose daughter Nicole became Dan's stepsister. His father married Lisa. Danny spent time with both families. On Tuesday, April 20, Danny's father Brian knew something was wrong when his son failed to show up at the shop after school like normal. His family agonized for hours waiting to find out what happened to their son. They learned the truth when Sue saw

COLUMBINE NOW

the Rocky Mountain News on the morning of Wednesday the 21st. She recognized her son's body in a heart-breaking photo.

Sue didn't often see Dan in the mornings but the morning of April 20th, they managed to come together for a brief chat that ended with a hug, a kiss, and her telling him she loved him. For months he had forgotten to bring home his school pictures from fall. That morning, he pulled one out of his backpack and gave it to her.

He was known in the media reports later as "the boy who held the door open" for friends, allowing them to escape from the school during the assault. It's a heroic notion but it isn't supported by the evidence or witness statements. Chances are his story was confused with that of Sean Graves, who was stuck in the doorway of the cafeteria, paralyzed. Regardless, the people who knew him all agreed on one thing: Danny was a wonderful young man who would be sorely missed.

Sue Petrone wants some good to come from her son's death; a less-violent world. In December 1999 she and husband Rich were treated to a video recording of Danny being interviewed in 1998 while sitting on the stairs on the southwest side of Columbine. They had never seen the footage. Ironically, he was wearing the same shirt he was wearing when he was killed on April 20th. The video came from a tape that Bethanee Scott found when she and her family were looking through their home videos. Bethanee is the sister of victim Rachel Scott, who likely filmed the interview. When Bethanee recognized Danny, she called Sue. She and Rich hurried over to see the tape. The videos the Petrones had of Danny were taken when he was younger. The video footage they received from Bethanee was "the best Christmas present ever".

Danny's funeral was held at Grace Presbyterian Church, and he was buried in Littleton Cemetery in Littleton, Colorado. Brian and Lisa Rohrbough adopted two kids from Ukraine, Rachel and Isaac, on September 9, 2003.

Rachel Scott

Born August 5, 1981, Rachel Scott was a vibrant 17-year-old and straight-forward individual. A junior at Columbine, she wasn't afraid to stand up for what she believed in, no matter what. She played the lead in the school play, *The Smoke in the Room*, written by student Andrew Robinson and co-starring Rachel's friends Nick Baumgart, Lauren Beachem, and others. She was writing a play for her senior year about a piano player in the '20's who makes his own music in an impromptu fashion because he can't read music. Despite his talent, he took it for granted then lost everything. Her friend Sarah Arzola said that Rachel wrote music the same way.

Rachel also liked photography, produced her own videos, and dreamed of being a film director. She was "made for the camera" according to her father, Darrell, and was an aspiring writer and actress. She quit smoking at the request of friend Nick Baumgart who later took her to the prom. If she hadn't quit, it's quite possible she would've been at "Smoker's Pit" during lunch instead of the first victim.

Rachel was always close with her brother Craig but had trouble connecting with her father in the months before the shooting. The last week before her death, Rachel and her dad had a long and bonding discussion, something that left both feeling incredibly happy. For Darrell that moment would give him comfort when dealing with Rachel's death.

Throughout her life Rachel was an incredibly spiritual person. She was active in the Celebration Christian Fellowship church and the Orchard Road Christian Center. She often wrote to God in her diaries about wanting to "reach the unreached". She begged Him for the chance to show others the way, to let her life have some purpose in spreading His word. In 1998 she drew a collage of images that included a rose growing out of a columbine, with several dark drops spiraling around it. On the morning of the shootings, she doodled a reprise of the picture: a pair of eyes crying thirteen teardrops onto that same rose – the same number of victims the shooters killed during the massacre just a couple of hours later.

After her death, Rachel's car was turned into a makeshift memorial by her friends where it sat in the parking lot. They hugged the fenders and kissed the windows. Huddled together, they began to chant: "We are COLUMBINE! We are COLUMBINE!"

"In my eyes, she was just one of those kinds of people you know you won't ever meet again," Rachel's friend Lauren Beachem said of her. *"She was the kind of person only born once."*

Rachel was buried at Chapel Hill Memorial Gardens in the Columbine Memorial Garden in Littleton, Colorado.

Isaiah Shoels

Isaiah Shoels was born August 4, 1980. He was an 18-year-old a senior at Columbine. He was born with a congenital heart defect that required two surgeries when he was a child. He wanted to be a comedian, dreamed of becoming a music executive. After graduating he wanted to attend an arts college. Friends nicknamed him "Bushwick". Born with a heart defect, his parents said he was a fighter who overcame his disability and went on to play football and wrestle. He had played cornerback the previous year on the football team, but his father said he quit the team due to racial intimidation.

Isaiah also played keyboards and wanted to become a record producer, like his father Michael who was the president of Notorious Records and Ft. Knox Entertainment - a firm Michael started to promote black musicians in the Denver area. After graduation Isaiah had planned to attend the Denver Institute of the Arts.

Isaiah was a popular boy; Columbine principal Frank DeAngelis said his classmates would compete to work on school projects with him. *"Isaiah Shoels, thank you for having such a positive impact on our school and on our family. You will be greatly missed, and I love you, my dear child,"* he said at Isaiah's funeral.

"He's smiling down on us," classmate and friend Nick Foss said. *"I know he is."*

Isaiah was the only person of color who was killed at Columbine. He was due to graduate that May and wanted to attend art college.

Isaiah's brother Anthony was a freshman at Columbine and was outside with a friend when the shooting started. He was able to get to safety by running through the school and out the other side.

The last of the Columbine victims to be buried, Isaiah was laid to rest in Fairmount Cemetery in Denver, Colorado. Martin Luther King III, son of Martin Luther King, Jr., spoke at Isaiah's funeral at the Heritage Christian Center.

John Tomlin

Born September 1, 1982, John Tomlin was a 16-year-old sophomore at Columbine when he was killed in the library. A native of Wisconsin, his family moved to Littleton in 1995 when his father John Michael got a job there with a heating firm. Shy and lonely, John found the move difficult at first. He soon made friends with Jacob Youngblood and Brandon Sokol, both of whom later spoke at his funeral.

John attended the Foothills Bible Church and belonged to the Riverside Baptist Church South youth group where he met his girlfriend of seven months, Michelle Oetter. His sister Ashley said the pair were nearly inseparable.

"He treated me like the queen of the world," Michelle said of John.

COLUMBINE NOW

John loved church and Chevrolet trucks. He had recently got his driver's license and had just bought an old Chevy pickup that he had been working for since he was 14. He enjoyed off-roading in the Rocky Mountains. He once drove all the way to Mexico to help build a house for a poor family. He enjoyed four-wheeling in his truck and lifting weights.

He was gentle and kind. Family and friends remember his energy and the warmth of his smile. *"He had such a sense of humor. He was always making goofy faces,"* his mother said.

He worked after school and on weekends at Arapahoe Acres Nursery hauling trees and driving tractors 30 hours a week. According to friends, he always wore the same thing to work: Carpenter pants, mud-caked boots, a blue cap, and a jacket featuring his favorite team, the Green Bay Packers. He planned to join the army when he graduated. His truck, like Rachel Scott's car, became a standing memorial in the parking lot. Thursday following the shootings, his family gathered around the truck even though it was raining. His bible was still sitting on the dashboard, where he always left it in the hope that someone would see something there that would bring them closer to God. His grandfather, John Francis, his father, and other family members took turns sitting in the truck. John's father said of him:

"He was as close to a perfect son as you could get. He was just good. You'd ask him to wash a car, and he'd wash both cars."

John spent his lunch hour in the library every day studying. He was there when the gunmen stormed the school. Hiding under a table, he welcomed a girl he didn't know (victim Nicole Nowlen) into his hiding place when she grew too scared to stay where she was hiding. He held her hand to comfort her when the killers started shooting people in the library. When he heard one of the gunmen harassing victim Valeen Schnurr after she'd been shot, John confronted the shooter. The bold move got him killed.

The first of the funerals for the victims killed at Columbine, his was held at Foothills Bible Church where he had attended church. He was buried in his hometown of Waterford, Wisconsin, in Saint Peters Cemetery. He was buried in a satin-lined coffin of green and gold, the colors of his favorite team, embroidered with Chevy trucks.

A while after his death his family found his "to do" list for fixing up his truck. You can find out about how they got it fixed up in Sean Reavie's book *Keys to the Kingdom*.

Lauren Townsend

Born January 17, 1981, 18-year-old Lauren Townsend was a senior and captain of the girls' varsity volleyball team, which her mother, Dawn Anna, coached. She was a member of the National Honor Society and was a candidate for valedictorian of her graduating class. Lauren was a talented sketch artist as well. Nicknamed "Lulu" she was a straight 'A' student; she never got a 'B'. She volunteered at a local animal shelter and had planned to major in biology at Colorado State University when she graduated from Columbine.

Lauren was in the library with her friends Lisa Kreutz, Diwata Perez, Valeen Schnurr, and Jeanna Park when the shooting began. She hid beneath the table with them when the teacher told everyone to get down. Val Schnurr was beside her, shaking with terror. Lauren put her arm around her, drew her close and told her everything would be okay.

Lauren's funeral was held at Foothills Bible Church where her brother Josh played a tribute video filled with moments from her life. Many of her teachers spoke at her funeral, commending her gentle nature and loving spirit as well as her academic excellence. Her coffin was a white one that people attending her funeral could write on, much like one would sign a yearbook. Her father wrote: *"Lulu, you'll always be my baby."*

COLUMBINE NOW

She was buried in Littleton Cemetery in Littleton, Colorado.

At the groundbreaking ceremony of the Columbine Memorial, the day had been stormy while Dawn Anna gave a moving speech that began with: *"They're here. Can you feel them? Our angels."* At the end of the event, the clouds parted, and a beautiful rainbow appeared over Rebel Hill. Principal Frank DeAngelis has a picture of that rainbow at Columbine.

Kyle Velasquez

Born May 5, 1989, Kyle Velasquez was a 16-year-old sophomore at Columbine. Neighbors and relatives say Kyle enjoyed chores and family activities. They say he was a "gentle giant" who saw the good in people. A sophomore, he was six feet tall and 230 pounds when he died but those who knew him knew that he was a little boy at heart. Affectionate and sincere, he loved nothing more than helping his dad, Albert, out around the house: Putting up shelves, mowing the lawn, washing the car. Every day he would kiss his mom, Phyllis, on the cheek and tell her that he loved her. He loved his brother Daniel and the family cats. He enjoyed playing with computers and eating ice cream. He dreamed of joining the Navy like his dad or becoming a firefighter.

When Kyle was a baby, he suffered a stroke that left him mentally disabled, and he also had severe asthma. As a "special needs" child, Kyle was often ignored, avoided, and teased while growing up – he knew what it was like to be an outcast. Due to his disabilities, Kyle's parents were prepared to spend the rest of their lives with him. He accompanied his mother everywhere while she ran her errands. Kyle's last words to her were: *"Goodbye. I love you, mom."*

A shy teen, Kyle had only been attending Columbine for three months and was just beginning to come out of his shell when the massacre occurred. It was only a few weeks that he was staying at the school through lunch; a few weeks earlier and he would've been on his way home the day the shooting started.

Friends and relatives brought food, hugs, and love to the Velasquez home following the shooting. They described the family as tight knit.

Kyle was buried with full military color guard honors in Fort Logan National Cemetery in Denver, Colorado, since his father was a Navy veteran. His parents were given the flags from his coffin and the one that was flown at half-mast in Kyle's honor at the state Capitol.

Coach William "Dave" Sanders

Born October 22, 1951, 47-year-old William "Dave" Sanders was a computer and business teacher at Columbine for 25 years, and coach of the girls' basketball and softball teams. He left behind his wife, four children and five grandchildren.

His students said he was a teacher, a friend, a mentor, and an inspiration. He was good friends with the other coaches and with Principal Frank DeAngelis, who he assisted back when DeAngelis was Columbine's baseball coach.

When the gunmen opened fire outside the school he ran through the cafeteria and sounded the alarm. He, along with two of the school's janitors, helped get hundreds of students out of the path of danger by herding them away from the shooters. His quick actions saved untold numbers of lives that day.

By the time the gunmen arrived, the cafeteria was nearly empty. Sanders was in the upstairs hall trying to get students safely hidden in classrooms when he was gunned down. With assistance from teacher Rich Long, he managed to get to a science lab. Despite first aid from students and teachers, Sanders bled to death while waiting for emergency assistance that took too long to arrive.

COLUMBINE NOW

Dave's daughter Angela said at his funeral: *"What you did in that school on Tuesday was an amazing act of heroism. Even after you were hurt, you continued to be the brave, selfless man we all know you are."*

Dave was buried in Littleton's Chapel Hill Memorial Gardens. Since his death, Coach Dave Sanders has had a softball field at Columbine and a scholarship named after him to honor his memory and posthumously received the Arthur Ashe Award for Courage. A highway also bears his name.

THE INJURED

In deference to their privacy, I have not included the birthdates of the following individuals. I have only included information I thought was relevant to the focus of this book. I wish all of the stories were success stories, but they're not. However, every single person who was injured has truly tried to go on with life as best they could.

You can find more information about their experiences during the school and the nature of their injuries at aColumbineSite.com, but this book tries to highlight how they survived and prevailed against the odds stacked against them as well as the strides they have made on their roads to recovery.

Brian Anderson

Brian was inside the school, heading for the west entrance with a friend when he was shot at. He was injured but managed to escape to the library where he hid in the periodicals room of the library until he could escape.

Brian was treated for injuries sustained from bullet fragments bouncing off a shattering window when Eric shot through the double-paned west-entrance doors. He was released April 20, 1999. He graduated from Columbine on May 20, 2000.

85

In 2008 a friend of Brian's, Dewayne Johnson, said Brian Anderson had moved on with his life. He owned his own trucking company in the Littleton, Colorado area. Brian was still trying to make sense of what happened that fateful day at Columbine High School. Up to that point he still hadn't stepped one foot into any library, nor did he like the sound of helicopters or fire alarms.

Brian lost his good friend Corey DePooter in the shooting and said there were times when he thought of him and all the fun times they had in school. Brian said "there is one person that means a lot" to him and will always have a place in his heart because in his eyes she was a HERO: Patti Nielson.

Richard Castaldo

Richard was friends with Rachel Scott. They were seated on the grassy knoll outside the west entrance of the school when the shooting began. He and Rachel had recently started eating lunch together every other day. They were doing just that when the shooters opened fire on them.

Richard played dead until law enforcement came to pull him off the grass. He was the last of the injured to be released from the hospital. He remains in a wheelchair.

He got his driver's license in February 2000, and drove a van modified for his wheelchair. He was featured in Michael Moore's *Bowling for Columbine* film wherein he, along with Mark Taylor, managed to convince K-mart to stop selling ammunition. It came out later that Moore was less than honest with Richard and the other survivors regarding his intentions with the film but at least some good came from his involvement with it.

In 2000, Castaldo's father Rick made a congressional testimony about Project Exile: The Safe Streets and Neighborhoods Act of 2000. According to his statement, he and Richard didn't blame the guns for what happened. They also didn't feel that making more laws would help as over 17 federal laws were already broken during the shootings at Columbine High. Instead, they wanted the government to focus on prosecuting to the full extent laws that were already in place.

On January 31, 2002, the Olympic torch was passed along Pierce Street, from survivor Patrick Ireland to Richard Castaldo and Columbine principal Frank DeAngelis. DeAngelis handed it off to John Tomlin Sr, father of victim John Tomlin.

May 6, 2006 Richard was interviewed by Kotaku about his opinions regarding the Super Columbine Massacre RPG!, which he downloaded and played to see exactly what it was. In his words:

"I appreciate the fact at least to some degree that something like this was made. I think that at least it gets people talking about Columbine in a unique perspective, which is probably a good thing. But that being said there are a lot of things that are hard to play or watch. And it seems to partially glamorize what happened."

Director Danny Ledonne put out a documentary film in 2008 called *Playing Columbine* that Richard Castaldo was featured in regarding the subject of the game and the Columbine shootings.

In 2020, Richard lost his apartment after succumbing to a bad infection, but a team of volunteers helped keep him fed and sheltered and helped him search for a new home. He told the LA Times:

"I guess everyone wonders why Columbine happened and I don't know, frankly. I think America is part of the problem. The American culture is so violent. I think when Trump said he could shoot someone on Fifth Avenue and not lose any supporters, I think that right there capsulizes everything that's wrong with America to me. I think that's the bottom-line sickness of America right there. As if shooting someone is some kind of joke."

In 2023, Richard worked in the music department on the film *The Uncanny*.

Jennifer Doyle

Jennifer was sitting at a table in the library when teacher Patti Nielson hollered for everyone to get down. She was going to get under the table she shared with Mark Kintgen, but she was concerned it wasn't big enough to hide her. So, she ran to a table toward the back of the library where she hid with Peter Ball, Austin Eubanks, and Corey DePooter. Corey told her and Austin that everything was going to be all right.

Jennifer had her hand on Corey's shoulder when one of the gunmen opened fire on their table. She was injured by the blast but survived and was able to escape along with Austin. She was released from the hospital on April 24, 1999. Jennifer now has a metal plate and screws holding her ring finger together. She graduated from Columbine High School on May 20, 2000, and went on to attend the University of Colorado that fall.

Stephen "Austin" Eubanks

Austin was with his best friend Corey DePooter in the library when the shooting began. When the teacher ran in telling everyone to get down, he, Corey, Jennifer Doyle, and Peter Ball hid under the same table.

"Everything's going to be okay," Corey told them.

When the shooters finally left the library, Austin and the other survivors got up and ran outside where they were met by police officers who shuttled him to triage for his injuries. Austin was released from the hospital the same day and graduated from Columbine High School on May 20, 2000.

In May 2019, shortly after the 20th anniversary of the shooting, Austin died from an accidental heroin overdose. He struggled with opioid addiction that he developed due to his injuries at Columbine. Before his death, Austin was a powerful public speaker who touched many hearts with his talks at conferences, graduations, and through online videos.

COLUMBINE NOW

Nicholas 'Nick' Foss

Nick was in the cafeteria eating lunch when he heard a girl shout: "Someone's shooting! Someone's shooting!" He and his friend Tim Kastle hid in the teachers' lounge bathroom with Joyce Jankowski and three other school employees.

According to statements Nick gave investigators, he suggested they should try to escape through the ceiling ventilation shaft. Ms. Jankowski tried first only to fall through the ceiling. Tim tried next and was able to get out. Nick went up next and tried to escape by crawling through the ceiling but fell through into the lounge. He was able to run from the building to police officers waiting outside.

He had a twin brother, Adam, who was also in the school at the time of the shootings. Trapped in an office, Adam helped other students up into the ceiling where the air wasn't so stuffy so they could breathe easier while they hid.

Nick was treated for injuries and released April 20, 1999. He graduated from Columbine in May 1999.

Sean Graves

Sean was heading up the hill outside of Columbine's west entrance with his friends Dan Rohrbourgh and Lance Kirklin when they were fired on. He almost made it to the cafeteria before he was hit. He spent a long time lying in the doorway of the cafeteria, too injured to move.

Sean was best friends with fellow victim Patrick Ireland. Since the shooting, Sean and Lance Kirklin haven't spoken much about that day. Sean said he gets too emotional to talk to Lance in person, preferring email correspondence as of 1999.

Sean's back/spine injury was deemed an 'incomplete spinal injury' by doctors, meaning that he was paralyzed below the injury level but retained some feeling and movement. He was later moved to Craig Hospital for spinal cord rehabilitation. On

June 20th, 1999, he took his first steps. He was released from Craig Hospital on July 7th, 1999.

Sean told reporters he used to have nightmares about being shot long before the attack on Columbine. Those nightmares stopped after the shooting. His home was rebuilt to accommodate the wheelchair he was using at the time. Donations from people around the world paid for a home gym to assist with his personal therapy. Sean's father Randy purchased him a used pick-up truck when Sean was 16, when the teen proved to his father he could get in and out of it unassisted.

Sean graduated from Columbine in 2002, using only a crutch to walk across the stage to receive his diploma. That same year Sean went back to Columbine for the 5th anniversary of the tragedy. He planned to place a cigar on the ground where Danny died. He said:

"Watching my friend die is still traumatic, but it is in the past. I'm not trying to be mean. I just have to focus on today and looking at the positive and the future."

As of 2023, Sean was married to longtime girlfriend Kara and had a daughter, Olivia. He still lived just six miles from Columbine. When asked if he ever considered moving, he told the interviewers: *"No. This is my home."*

Makai Hall

Makai was sitting with his friends in the library when the shooting began. He hid under a table with Daniel Steepleton and Patrick Ireland when the shooters entered the library. When they demanded that everyone with white hats stand up, Dan – who was wearing a white hat – started to get up. Makai held him back, telling him: *"Don't move."*

Shortly after that, one of the gunmen fired at their table. When one of them threw a home-made CO_2 bomb under their table Makai threw it back out. It exploded mid-air.

Three days after the tragic event he was interviewed by CNN. He was quite modest when asked to discuss his act of heroism.

He underwent surgery and spent 3 days in the hospital. He was released April 23, 1999. He graduated from Columbine on May 20, 2000. He studied business finance at Colorado State University, where he met his wife on the first day. He decided to pursue a career in healthcare because of the kindness shown to him by those who helped him. He got a job working as a nurse with UCHealth where his coworkers provided him comfort.

Makai told UCHealth in a 2019 interview:

"If you find yourself after an experience like this or having experienced violence in a bad place, it's not hopeless. There's a way to kind of come back to the light."

In 2019, Makai was featured in the Rocky Mountain PBS documentary *Ripples of Columbine*. He was married and had three children.

Anne Marie Hochhalter

Anne Marie was outside eating lunch on the grassy knoll with her friends when the shooting began. Her 16-year-old brother Nathan was also a student at Columbine and was in one of the Science rooms at the time. She was paralyzed by a bullet that severed her spinal cord. When she was rescued by paramedic John Aylward, she had virtually no blood pressure. If rescue hadn't reached her when they did, she would have died. Doctors called her the "miracle girl".

Anne Marie spent a total of four months in the hospital. At Craig Hospital she underwent rehabilitative therapy with fellow survivor Patrick Ireland. She resumed school September 9, 1999, and had one Physics class with him. Her family bought a house with wheelchair ramps and lifts with the help of the Colorado Homebuilders Foundation. At age 18, she was attending

Columbine part time and helped in the nurse's office in addition to taking classes. She wanted to go on to community college once she graduated but planned to take the summer of 2000 off to "be a teen" since she'd lost that time the previous summer.

The following is Anne Marie's open letter to the public the day she was released from the hospital and is unedited:

"To all the people who have cared about me from the day I was hurt:

I am leaving Craig Hospital today and didn't want to have a press conference but wanted to write my own press release. I have wanted to be private during my recovery, and I appreciate the media's respect for my wishes.

I have many thanks to share. First, I wish to thank my family who has loved and supported me all through my recovery. I would like to thank the paramedics and staff at Swedish Medical Center who saved my life. I want to thank the Craig Hospital staff who taught me the skills to be independent again. I want to thank my many friends who have visited me and cared about my well-being from the very beginning.

Thanks also to the families who have brought meals to my family every night, and to all the caring people across the country who prayed for me, and who sent wonderful gifts and cards. They meant a lot to me. Your loving care and support have helped me tremendously to get through my recovery.

I still have many obstacles to overcome, but I know that I can do it, and God will give me strength along the way.

Once again, I give my thanks to all of you."

Anne Marie Hochhalter

August 12, 1999

Just two months later her family in the news again following the suicide of her mother, Carla Hochhalter. Anne Marie's mother had struggled with depression for at least three years before the shooting. Following the shooting, people who knew Carla (including Richard Castaldo's mother Connie Michalik) said they saw how much the tragedy affected her.

Anne Marie's father Ted was married to Carla for 22 years. A year after Carla's death, he married Katherine Zocco, who had been his grief counselor. Ted became a school safety activist who trained parents in how to respond to a crisis.

Anne Marie earned her business degree from the University of Colorado and bought a townhouse in Westminster. In 2002 she was working as a manager for the Westminster Bath & Body Works. She was promoted to Manager in 2009.

Patrick Ireland

Patrick was in the library at the time of the attack and was shot while trying to render first aid to Makai Hall. Pat passed in and out of consciousness for two hours on the floor of the library. The fire alarm finally woke him. He didn't know where he was or what was happening. He just knew he had to get out of there.

Badly injured, he was eventually able to pull himself up onto the ledge of a broken window. He rolled himself out into the arms of SWAT members who had gathered below to catch him. The rescue was captured by news crews and Pat was dubbed "the boy in the window" who survived the shooting against all odds.

He was treated for his injuries at multiple hospitals and rehab clinics. He returned to Columbine High that fall, using a cane to help support his weight as he walked. On September 25, 1999, he was elected Columbine's homecoming king. He graduated from Columbine on May 20, 2000, as a co-valedictorian. In 2004, Jefferson County reached a $117,500 settlement with Patrick Ireland though they assumed no liability settling the lawsuit.

In 2009 Pat was doing well for himself: He was working as a financial rep and had married sweetheart Kacie. By 2012, he had 2 daughters and moved up to managing director for Northwestern Mutual Financial Network. He, like many survivors, became a public speaker. He spoke at the 2019 National Summit on School Safety hosted by the Safe and Sound Schools organization.

Michael Johnson

Michael was outside the cafeteria with his friends Denny Rowe, Mark Taylor, John Cook, and Adam Thomas. They were sitting on the grass near the east stairs when the shooting began. Mike tried to run, but he was hit. He made it to a hiding spot behind the maintenance shed where he remained. Evan Todd and Ryan Barrett eventually joined him and tried to help him. A short time later he was removed from the shed area by law enforcement who then transported him to paramedics.

Though doctors thought he might lose his leg at one point Mike can now run and has held a job at the Mann Theater. His parents Kathy and Gary felt that though they went through a lot, the ordeal made them closer as a family.

Mike was in intensive care for 8 days. He was released April 28, 1999.

Mike served an LDS mission in California and studied at the Metropolitan State College of Denver. In 2004, Mike's story was published in the book *Surviving Columbine* (Deseret Book) along with those of Liz and Kathy Carlston and Amber Huntington, all of whom belong the Church of Jesus Christ of Latter-day Saints. The message the book conveys is that you shouldn't be surprised by the problems you can handle with the support of God. Mike told Deseret.com:

"You don't realize what you can go through until you have to," said Johnson. "It's all about doing what you have to do to get through. Trials change you. You can't go into a trial and leave unchanged — for better or worse. That's your choice."

COLUMBINE NOW

Joyce Jankowski

When the shooting began Joyce, a teacher at Columbine, was in the faculty lounge. She hid in the bathroom with three other staff members. Three students (Nick Foss, Tim Kastle, and Sean Nossaman) soon joined them. At one point, Tim Kastle headed up into the ceiling to try to escape. Joyce followed, but she fell through the acoustic tile and hurried back to the bathroom.

About 40 minutes after the attack began, a student's head appeared in the open spot in the ceiling where Tim had gone out. The student up in the ceiling told the group that they should "run off now".

Joyce and the others ran through the cafeteria and out the northwest door to a police unit stationed near the school.

She was treated for injuries sustained in the fall through the ceiling when she tried to escape the school and was released April 20, 1999.

Mark Kintgen

Assigned to "B" lunch, Mark's 5th period was a free period, and he usually spent it in the library. He was there when the shooters entered the library.

Mark later remembered hearing a male voice asking someone: "Do you believe in God?". The next thing he remembered was waking up covered in splinters, afraid he was going to die. He crawled out from under the table and followed Patti Blair out of the library to the safety of the patrol cars positioned outside of the school.

He was treated and released from Denver Health on April 23, 1999.

Mark has cerebral palsy. He has a twin brother named Mike who also attended Columbine. His mother, Kay, hopes that they will one day find closure. Mark graduated on May 20, 2000.

He got his bachelor's degree at Colorado State University with a Major in History and a Minor in Business. He was in the CSU Marketing Club for 3 years. He works as a Library Assistant at the University of Denver.

Lisa Kreutz

Lisa usually spent her "A" lunch period either in the library or going out to lunch with friends Jessica Holliday and Bethany Koch. On April 20th she sat with Jessica, Jeanna Park, and Diwata Perez on the east side of the library. She joined Jessica, Jeanna, Diwata, and Lauren Townsend. When the shooting started, she hid under the table with her friends and another girl she didn't know, Kelly Fleming.

She was severely injured by gunfire and was too injured to leave, eventually rescued by officials. She was the last survivor to be pulled from the library.

Lisa was released from the hospital April 28, 1999. She graduated from Columbine High on May 23, 1999, wheeled to the podium with a cast on her leg and a sling on her arm, her parents Ken and Sheryl Kreutz in attendance. She later attended the University of Colorado. She has never spoken publicly about what happened to her in the library on April 20, 1999.

Lance Kirklin

Lance had "A" Lunch with Dan Rohrbough and Sean Graves. He was shot on the stairs outside when the three of them left the cafeteria to head to Smoker's Pit so he could have a cigarette.

Lance was gravely injured. He underwent 9 operations over the course of three years. He was due to have more, but procedure fatigue and the pending birth of his first child made him decide to quit in 2001.

COLUMBINE NOW

He was released from St. Anthony Central Hospital on May 15, 1999. On May 21 he went with investigators to Columbine to do a walk-through of the crime scene in hopes of remembering more details about that tragic day. He returned to Columbine the next school year but was suspended due to sporadic attendance. He continued to hunt with his dad Mike and spoke up for gun rights April 2000 at a Denver town meeting about guns which was attended by President Bill Clinton. He and his father moved into a new house with their new puppy Hunter.

In 2019, Lance was featured in the Rocky Mountain PBS *Ripples of Columbine* documentary.

Letter from Lance Kirklin's family to the public:

"Lance has worked hard to overcome adversity. He believes in treating others as he would want to be treated. He is sensitive, caring and able to put the needs of others before his own. Though he is unable to speak at this time due to the nature of his injuries, he has indicated tremendous sadness and concern for the others affected by this tragedy. Knowing Lance, he would want to be available to comfort others and is moved by the outpouring of love and support he has received.

We know that Lance has many challenges to address, and we count on and ask for your continued prayers and support in the months ahead for all students and families affected.

Lance is an outdoorsman and loves to fish. He likes the opportunity to be in the mountains with family and friends. We know that his sadness will be lightened when he is again able to go to the mountains.

On behalf of Lance, we would like to thank all involved in Lance's rescue, Littleton and other communities throughout Colorado, across the country and worldwide for their prayers, support and love extended to Lance and his family. Especially all Lance's family in Scotts Bluff, Nebraska, we appreciate your prayers and love. We would also like to thank Denver Health administrators, Surgical Intensive Care staff, Emergency

Department staff, surgeons and everyone for caring for Lance and our family."

Dawn, Mike, and Amanda Kirklin

Adam Kyler

Adam was in the cafeteria when the shooting began with his friend Kyle Velasquez. They were both Special Needs students. Adam hid under his table when he heard Coach Dave Sanders yell for the students to get down. He was injured when he got up later to run to a better hiding place. A chair struck him in the chest. He got back to his feet with the help of his friend Dusty Hoffschneider and the two of them ran to the kitchen. Adam went into the storage area. Adam and 18 other people stayed hidden in the kitchen where they barricaded the doors. They stayed there till the SWAT team came to evacuate them.

When authorities asked Adam how he knew Dylan Klebold, Adam told them Dylan had harassed him at school in November and December 1998. It got so bad that Adam's mother, Susan Kyler, reported it to the school authorities who said they would take care of the problem. There were no further issues after that.

He was treated for abdominal pain at Centura Littleton Adventist Hospital and released April 20, 1999. In an interview after the shooting, Adam spoke about how Rachel Scott once stood up for him when he was being bullied.

Stephanie Munson

Stephanie had just transferred to Columbine 4 months before the shooting. She and her friend Melissa Walker were heading out of tech lab class to go talk with one of the A.C.E. teachers when she heard popping noises. Science teacher Frank Peterson ran up the hall leading a small herd of students, yelling at them to get out of the building. She and Melissa ran west toward the main entrance.

COLUMBINE NOW

As they were exiting through the first set of double doors Stephanie was shot in the foot.

Melissa helped her flee to Leawood Park where someone with a cellphone called 911. An ambulance arrived and took her to Centura Littleton Adventist Hospital where she was treated and released on April 20, 1999.

Stephanie and her younger sister Jennifer designed a commemorative Columbine stuffed bear to raise money and honor the victims. It was made available shortly after the shootings to raise money for other victims. One of the bears was put inside the shuttle Endeavor for an 11-day mission before it was presented back to Stephanie.

When classes resumed in fall of 1999, Stephanie returned to Columbine High.

Patricia 'Patti' Nielson

Patti Nielson, a substitute art teacher, was on hall monitor duty on April 20th, 1999. She was the first staff member at Columbine to encounter one of the gunmen. Mistaking the gun that he held for a toy one, she was injured when she stepped outside to tell him to get it off campus. She was responsible for alerting the students in the library to the coming danger. She placed a 9-11 call from the library that lasted over 20 minutes during which she repeatedly told the kids in the room to stay hidden.

Patti, a mother of 3 kids, finished out the rest of the school year when classes resumed at Chatfield and went back the first two months of the new school year at Columbine when it reopened in fall of 1999. Then she took a much-needed leave. While Patti eventually returned to teaching, she switched to teaching elementary classes at another school. She also continued to pursue her master's degree, though her focus had shifted to family-first. She didn't want her career path to come between her and time with her kids.

Patti was treated at Pierce Street triage for her injuries then she was then taken to the hospital where she was treated and released on April 20, 1999.

In 2004, Patti told NBC news: *"I can't change whatever went wrong with those boys. And I probably will never have an answer to what went wrong."*

Nicole Nowlen

Nicole had been attending Columbine for only six weeks before the shooting. When her dad enrolled her at the high school, he told her he was sending her there because he knew she would be safe there. It was the school he had attended as a teen. Nicole was assigned to "A" lunch but she typically spent that time in the library or an empty classroom so she could do homework. She was in the library the morning of April 20th.

When teacher Patti Nielson came in and told everyone to get down, Nicole hid under her table. But she didn't feel safe there. A nearby table offered better concealment but there was already a boy hiding there. She asked him if she could join him. John Tomlin checked the library entrance then waved her over. They pulled chairs in around themselves for better concealment.

As the sound of gunfire got closer John held her hand to comfort her. Doctors later called her the "miracle girl" because she survived a close-range shotgun. She was treated at Lutheran Medical Center and released with five shotgun pellets still in her body on April 21, 1999.

She went back to Columbine after she recovered, refusing to let Eric and Dylan "win" by chasing her out of her school. She took on a part-time job at an appliance store in her junior year and did reach-out work for the Rachel's Challenge movement.

In 2001, she moved to Nashville, Tennessee where she worked as a medical transcriber. By 2003, Nicole was living in Franklin, Tennessee where she was a circulation assistant for

Board Member Magazine. In 2006, the organization Rachel's Challenge brought her on part time to help spread their mission of compassion and kindness, Nicole spoke at events all over the USA and Canada. By 2007 she was working for the organization full-time and had spoken at over 80 schools about her experience.

She told one audience about how when she arrived at the emergency room on April 20th, a doctor told her the probable reason she survived was because she was overweight, which stopped the shotgun pellets from reaching any vital organs. She laughed about it, saying: *"You see? The thing you dislike the most about yourself may just be the thing that saves your life."*

Her mother Shawna Anderson said of Nicole: *"I am very proud of her. Nicole had a bad situation, and she turned it into a way to help other people."*

Jeanna Park

Jeanna was hiding under a table in the library with Lauren Townsend, Lisa Kreutz, Diwata Perez, and Valeen Schnurr during the shooting. Her friends had to hold her back because her younger sister Kathy was hiding somewhere else in the room, and she wanted to be sure she was okay. Jeanna was nearly killed when she was shot repeatedly. Despite her critical injuries, Jeanna was able to muster the strength to escape from the library after the gunmen left the room.

She was released from Denver Medical Center on April 26, 1999. Jeanna returned to Columbine when she was well enough. She graduated with honors on May 23, 1999, still wearing a sling on her right arm.

Kacey Ruegsegger

Kacey was in the library reading when the shooting began. She hid under a table in the computer lab, in a cubby between Steve Curnow and Amanda Stair. She miraculously survived a point-blank shotgun blast. After the gunmen left the room, students Craig Scott and Sarah Houy helped her up. She managed to make it out of the building and to the police waiting outside where she was rushed off to the triage area.

Kacey had transferred to Columbine a few months before the shooting after suffering the loss of four friends. Her parents wanted her to be in a more positive environment. Kacey underwent several surgeries and lengthy physical therapy due to her injuries. She was released from the St. Anthony Central Hospital on May 1, 1999. She went on to attend Colorado State University. Kacey eventually married and had children of her own. Though sending them to school has been difficult, she knows it's best for their development that she not let her trauma keep them from living a full life. Kacey became a public speaker and has spoken at several events.

She wrote a book, *Over My Shoulder: A Columbine Survivor's Story of Resilience, Hope, and a Life Reclaimed*, which was published Mar. 22, 2019. It's her hope that by sharing her story, others will find purpose and healing in their own lives. She told Denver7 in an interview that year that it took her 20 years to come to terms with what happened to her. That's when she made the choice not to let the event haunt her forever.

Following the Uvalde shooting in 2022, her message to the survivors was that they somehow had to "turn pain into purpose" by finding hope in tomorrow.

Valeen Schnurr

Valeen was in the library during the shootings. When she was shot, she cried out "Oh, my God!", which prompted one of the gunmen to ask her if she believed in God. It was initially reported that Cassie Bernall was the one who was asked this question, and that she died because she said "yes". When Salon.com finally set the record straight, Val came under a lot of social pressure. People she didn't know accused her and her family of lying, calling her a copycat. Val wasn't interested in martyrdom though and never pushed anyone to give up their ideal of Cassie, especially not Cassie's parents. Mark and Shari Schnurr, Valeen's parents, found it difficult but they understood the situation was complicated. Val was spiritual enough to know it didn't matter. If Cassie's example brought others to God or gave them comfort, that's all that mattered to her. She preferred to try to live life as normally as possible rather than be known as a hero.

When Misty Bernall published her book about Cassie, the Bernalls asked to meet with the Schnurrs. Shari could see it was Misty's way of healing. The Bernalls asked if they could include information about Valeen. Val agreed only to a brief mention. The book doesn't dwell on Cassie's death but instead focuses on the struggles she went through before the shooting.

Val was treated at Swedish Hospital for her grave injuries, released on April 27. She graduated from Columbine on May 23, 1999. That fall she started college at the University of North Colorado with a Major in Psychology.

Daniel Steepleton

Daniel was in the library with his friends Makai Hall, Corey DePooter, Patrick Ireland, and Austin Eubanks when the shooting occurred. When teacher Patti Nielson came in and told everyone to get down, Dan hid under the table with Makai, Pat, and a dark-haired girl he didn't know. Corey and Austin ran to the back of the room to hide.

When the shooters were calling for jocks to stand up, Dan almost did. He thought they had seen his white hat – a symbol of being an athlete at Columbine – and didn't want his friends to get hurt. Makai stopped him. All three boys were injured during the shooting. Dan was able to escape, but he felt bad later because he couldn't help his friend Pat.

Dan was treated and released from the hospital before April 24, 1999. Daniel graduated from Columbine on May 20,

2000. He went on to teach Science in the Jefferson County Public School system from 2008-2012. In 2022, he was working as an Aerospace Instructor with Littleton Public Schools.

Mark Taylor

Mark had been attending Columbine for only three weeks when the shooting happened. He was one of the first victims, surviving incredible odds. He was treated and released April 30, 1999. He was later re-admitted for infection and was in and out of the hospital three times.

Mark never returned to Columbine, instead enrolling in Dove Christian School. He and his family created a "Ten Commandments Bear" to honor those who died during the massacre. In 2000, Mark spoke publicly about his experience. A born-again Christian, Mark spoke at several churches including Calvary Church and New Hope Church.

In 2001, he sued Solvay Pharmaceuticals on the grounds that their anti-depressant Luvox made Eric Harris psychotic and violent. His family also sued Harris and Klebold's parents. The Solvay suit was dropped in 2003. The suit against the Harris and Klebold families was settled in 2007.In 2002 Mark appeared in Michael Moore's film *Bowling for Columbine* along with Richard Castaldo and Brooks Brown. Together they successfully lobbied against K-mart to stop selling bullets to minors. Interviews with Mark later regarding the film show he wasn't entirely clear on what the movie would be about before he agreed to be in it. He said Moore used him and other Columbine victims for his own purposes then discarded them. In Mark's own words:

"I had no idea what Moore's agenda was. And he had an agenda. He had it all planned out, completely. I believe that every American has the right to have a gun. We should have the right to protect ourselves."

In 2006 Mark published his own book about his experiences of April 20, 1999: *I Asked, God Answered- A*

COLUMBINE NOW

Columbine Miracle. In 2008, Mark was put into The Lighthouse inpatient unit of Aspen Pointe hospital in Colorado Springs after an alleged meltdown at a bookstore. The actual reason behind his detention remains unclear but when he was released, Mark was not the same person. After two consecutive stays in the ward, he was unable to form coherent answers when he was interviewed in 2009. In 2021, friends of the family put together a GoFundMe to help Mark pay for his medical and living expenses.

Evan Todd

He was in the library with friends when the shooters came to the library. He was hiding behind a pillar when he was fired on by one of the gunmen. He ducked behind a copy counter to get out of the line of fire. He was safe for a few minutes, but later was face-to-face with both killers, who threatened him but ultimately let him live.

Evan escaped the school after they left, ending up behind a police unit with one of the friends he'd been with in the library. Though Evan had been injured when he was shot at, he helped provide first aid to victims who were in worse shape than he was. Eventually he was sent to a triage site, but he left on foot to go call his parents. Evan was never taken to the hospital though he did go to a nearby clinic where he was treated for abrasions. He was released the same day.

The last of the survivors to be identified; he was listed in Littleton papers as 'Unnamed Boy'. He returned to Columbine that fall and went on to play for the Columbine Rebels' state championship football team. He held a 27-10 wrestling record on the varsity squad and made Eagle Scout in 2000. At one point he wanted to become a law enforcement officer. He testified at the Colorado state house in favor of allowing people to carry guns on school grounds because he believes an armed teacher might have made the difference at Columbine. He has also done some public speaking on the topic. In 2019, Evan said: *"We need to respect the dignity of life and humans."*

UNINJURED SURVIVORS

While researching Columbine for the past 25 years, I've noticed that when the victims of the shooting are discussed in documentaries, on forums, and in news bits, those who survived the experience without physical harm are often forgotten. A handful have been noted here and there, but most are just names on an FBI list. At the memorial and support services that followed, many of them felt invisible. Some were even told by others that they were not victims because they had no physical wounds that could be seen.

There were nearly 2,000 students and staff at Columbine High that horrible day along with several hundred first responders. They all had to hunker down in fear and dodge bullets. They had to witness people get hideously wounded. They had to see people die. They saw their school and community torn to pieces by two disturbed killers. They were smothered under a blanket of media and onlooker attention. Even less coverage has gone to the trials the families went through. Parents and children were separated for long hours, not knowing if they would see each other again. Some never did.

Those who survived without physical injury have had their own tough roads to walk, often without support or understanding. Someone who saw their best friends shot and killed right beside them is going to have wounds inside no one can see. The impact on their families is even harder to gauge. Sometimes these soul injuries can take years to fully surface. And they never truly go away. But they have endured over the years and for most, they have come through to create positive change from the hardships they've been through.

I have spoken with a few of these people and have seen interviews with others. Many of them share a similar emotional ground where they, too, feel victimized but are reluctant to say as much either because they feel guilty or because of the reactions they've gotten when they did speak up. Everyone I've heard from deals with trauma-related issues due to the shooting. Yet because they weren't shot, their struggles are downplayed or forgotten.

Krista Hanley was in the cafeteria when the shooting started. A junior at the time, she didn't see anyone injured, though to her horror a friend who was hiding with her told her that the shooters were people she knew and considered friends. She later learned that the gunmen left two propane bombs just a few feet away from where she was. Fortunately, those bombs didn't go off as planned. After six months of therapy, the emergency funding for mental health services ran out for survivors. Hanley went into her first year of college with crippling anxiety. She wrestled with feelings of shame for having known the gunmen even though their actions would have killed her if the bombs had worked the way they wanted. A public speaker and an author now, Hanley pushes for better mental health services and a solution to the ongoing issue of gun violence in the United States.

Jami Amo was 15-year-old freshman who was also in the cafeteria when the shooting occurred. Neither her nor her older sister Stacey were injured during the assault. Following the tragedy, she believed nothing significant happened to her because they weren't hurt or killed. Over time she has come to understand just how much the experience has impacted her. She needs to know where all the exits of a building are. She doesn't go to theaters. She was diagnosed with post-traumatic stress disorder (PTSD) and experiences flashbacks when mass shootings happen. She sometimes suffers from panic attacks and anxiety. A mother of three, she is now a gun violence prevention advocate.

Twins Patti Blair and Kim (Blair) Woodruff were in different parts of the school during the shooting. Kim saw Danny Rohrbough killed and witnessed her friend Anne Marie Hochhalter get gunned down outside. Patti was in the library and was near the table where the gunmen killed John Tomlin. Both witnessed horrible things. Each had her own way of managing the stress that followed. Patti numbed her mind with violent films while Kim kept busy, to distract herself from the memories. Both dealt with flashbacks and struggled with the knowledge of the deaths that occurred near them. Ten years later, Kim was working as a teacher, and Patti was a computer programmer. Both had made great strides in their recovery, no longer experiencing flashbacks or survivors' guilt. Kim told NPR during the anniversary year:

"We can finally put it behind us and start seeing it as a piece of our lives and not having it be our lives."

Amanda Stair-Duran, sister to former Trench Coat Mafia member Joe Stair, was in the library during the shooting. She was the third person hiding under the southern computer lab table when the gunmen entered the room, right in line with victims Steve Curnow and Kacey Ruegsegger. She was right across from where Isaiah Shoels and Matt Kechter were killed. She could see Cassie Bernall from her hiding place. She made a series of YouTube videos in which she talks about her harrowing experience and the suicide of her brother in 2007. It's obvious from what she says that she has had quite a road of struggles due to what she lived through, but the video blogs gave her a cathartic outlet to express herself without a battery of questions from reporters. In 2019, she said that she was experiencing fewer panic attacks though she still deals with other physical ailments such as fibromyalgia.

Missy Mendo was 14 years old when the shooting happened. She got out of the building unharmed but slept between her parents that night, still wearing the shoes she'd worn at school that day because she wanted to be ready to run. Every year on April 20th she has trouble with her focus, leaving the fridge door open and misplacing her car keys. She relies on therapy and support from the Rebels Project. She now works with Heather Martin helping survivors of other tragedies.

Emily (Wyant) Olander was hiding under a library table with Cassie when Harris shot and killed her. Interviewed on scene that day, Emily told the reporter that witnessing her death was *"the worst feeling I've ever had"*. Unlike some of the survivors, Olander was able to avoid the pitfalls of substance abuse to manage her feelings after the shootings. She credits a strong support system for her recovery, saying: *"That's just how life is. You deal with it and handle it in a positive way. That's how you move forward and go on with the rest of your life."*

Diwata (Perez) Quach was also in the library during the shootings. She was under the table where Lauren Townsend and Kelly Fleming were killed. A senior at the time, Quach witnessed the death of her friend and saw several others injured. As a result of the extreme trauma, Diwata no longer remembers her high school years up until that point. She barely remembers her graduation. A fire alarm went off at an event and she flew into a panic, feeling like she was right back in the library of Columbine. Twenty years later she was still feeling survivors' guilt for not being able to help her friends and didn't have to go through the painful recovery those who were injured or who lost loved ones went through. It took her years to get to the point where she could let go of her anger and hatred to start healing. Her experience at Columbine eventually led her to become a nurse.

Andrew McDonald, a junior at Columbine in 1999, also copes with survivors' guilt. He was in Algebra class when the shooting began and was able to get out of the school safely. For years after, he wrestled with thoughts that he could have done more at the time. He also wonders if things had been changed in the United States on a policy level if things would have turned out differently for those in Parkland and other areas where there has been a mass shooting. He now works with people all over the world as a public speaker. He told Vox:

"I feel like I've tried to take what happened to us at Columbine and turn it into something positive."

COLUMBINE NOW

Over the 25 years since the shooting, a bigger Columbine family has banded together. It's a community that began naturally as a way for survivors to find strength together during the anniversary of the shooting. It has grown into a year-round support system for many. Staff members, former students, first responders, and their families can rely on those who share their experiences to be there when they need to talk to someone who can relate to what they are going through. It's the same sort of community I have seen in children's hospitals among parents who have terminal children. Though there is pain and suffering at the root, the ties that bind the individuals together focus on support, love, and understanding.

Everyone who was at Columbine that fateful day bears emotional scars that will never vanish. Most have said they can't stand the sound of fireworks and other loud, sudden sounds. Many don't feel comfortable in wide open spaces or in crowds. Fire alarms cause instant emotional breakdown for many who were trapped for hours in the school. Gunshots of any kind cause panic attacks. Even something as simple as seeing a police cruiser with lights flashing can be upsetting.

On a more positive note, all the people in the Columbine family whom I've spoken to have echoed the same idea: They want to take the negative and transform it into something positive for the future. Whether it's giving back to their community, making public speeches, writing books, educating children, or reaching out to troubled individuals in need of intervention, they are done with the dark shadows of the past. They are stepping into the light of a new chapter in life.

The Columbine Memorial is a monument to that ideal. It was established to honor the victims of the shooting and to give the public a place to remember them. It also stands for hope following tragedy. Lovingly constructed with symbols and emotional quotes, the memorial draws thousands of visitors every year. Maintained through private donations and grants, the site offers families a place for their loved ones to be remembered without having a bunch of strangers traipsing around the school or the cemeteries where they are buried.

Public interest in Columbine has waned only a little over the years. This is attributed to the relatability of the environment and the situation. Almost everyone can relate to some facet of the event, or some person. Anyone who spends any amount of time looking into the subject can't help but feel connected to it. And while there have unfortunately been some troubled individuals who have taken that influence the wrong direction, most people who are moved by the tragedy are inspired to do positive things with their feelings.

Because of the shooting, people many locations have worked together to develop readiness plans and charitable donation events. Groups and single individuals have worked hard to find ways to help. When Columbine was being renovated after the shooting, even kids in kindergarten got involved, saving their pennies to donate to the school. President Bill Clinton got personally involved as well, speaking directly to several of the staff of Columbine and going so far as to make a personal donation to fund the Columbine Memorial. Around the world, students and teachers have used the tragedy as the basis for essays and lessons, ensuring that the event and the people who experienced it are not forgotten.

COLUMBINE STAFF

It would be understandable if anyone who was at Columbine High that fateful day wanted to never return. Several students didn't. Out of the staff, however, Mr. De told me that most of them returned. A surprising number remain employed by the school or are heavily involved with it as volunteers in 2024.

Rich Long, the computer science teacher who helped Dave Sanders when he was shot, taught at Columbine for 28 out of his 30 years as an educator. After the shooting, he decided to change careers and went to work mowing the Homestead Golf Course. Long knew both shooters. Klebold had been his assistant at one time. But the day he saw them shoot Coach Sanders, he saw what he described as "true evil". He spent one more year at Columbine after the tragedy, then retired from education. Going back to teaching just didn't feel right to him. In 2019, he told the *Christian Science Monitor*:

"It was time for me to get out of that profession."

In contrast English teacher Kiki Leyba still works at Columbine as of 2024, teaching seniors. He said that the environment there over the past quarter of a century has helped him cope. Leyba never questioned whether he would go back to teaching at Columbine. He told *TIME* magazine:

"I love that place. It was not hard for me to go back."

In 2019, as the 20th anniversary of the shooting drew near, Leyba told his students what to expect of the day: More police than normal and other heightened safety measures. None of his students were even born when the shooting occurred. To that generation, the Columbine shooting was history, not life. They grew up in an age where mass shootings were all over social media. It's almost normalized news these days. On April 16th, 2019, when the news about Columbine-obsessed Sol Pais broke, Leyba's students were bombarded with concerned text messages from their families who feared a rampage. He allowed them to respond. Media crews armed with cameras were starting to show up outside the school, followed by even more law enforcement. It was an eerie reminder of that day in 1999. That same year, Leyba and his wife Kallie were featured in the documentary short film *Columbine 2024: 25 Years of Trauma* by director Jeff Vespa. Vespa also directed the 2020 documentary *Voices of Parkland*. Leyba said he hoped that the Columbine documentary would help others who've lived through traumatic events.

COLUMBINE NOW

Paula Reed is another teacher who returned to Columbine. Beginning in 1986, she taught English and was a dean there. When the fire alarm went off, she and her class followed protocol, thinking it was a drill. When students ran past her shouting "They've got guns!" she didn't believe it. Then came the sound of gunfire and explosions. At the back fence that surrounded Columbine, school administrators helped kids over. Reed saw backpacks, high heeled shoes, and other items pile up as the students left them behind. She later learned that two of the kids she coached on the forensics debate team, Rachel Scott and Daniel Mauser, were killed. While watching the news that night, she found out that one of the shooters was Dylan Klebold, whom she taught in his sophomore year. That was the last time she watched the news.

Reed worked through the next three years, to see the freshman class from 1999 through to graduation. She didn't want to abandon them, particularly the debate team whom she knew would be struggling with the loss of Mauser and Scott. Her third year back she suffered with health problems due to stress, so she took a 2-year leave of absence to recover and heal. She eased back into teaching after that.

After the Sandy Hook shootings, Reed and another teacher traveled to Connecticut to meet with and counsel the surviving teachers. She knew how important it was to let the survivors know that they would get through the horrific event. Reed said: *"We just want to come and offer hope. You're not alone. You can talk to other teachers that have been through this."*

One thing she hears a lot from survivors of shootings is "Is this normal?" when they are overwhelmed with emotion or suffer from memory loss. One survivor desperately wanted to "go back to normal". Reed's advice to survivors of tragedy:

"The old normal is gone... You will never have it again. So, kiss it goodbye. Whoever you were before this happened... you need to say goodbye to that person because they're gone

forever. You will come to love who this makes you, but it's going to take time."

Reed retired in 2018, with 32 years of educating to her credit. As of 2024, Reed was a member of the Jefferson County Schools Board of Directors District 2. Her term ends in 2025. She struggles with the fact that more hasn't been done over the years to tackle the subject of mass shootings.

There are other staff members who returned to Columbine and are still working there as of 2024 who didn't let their experiences deter them. Though they asked not to be referred to by name, they expressed their determination to continue to make a difference to honor the people who were injured and killed during the attack. Columbine is their home. It's their community and refuge. They actively support and care about one another.

In addition to these teachers, several people who were students at Columbine High in 1999 have stepped into the role of educator there. Mandy Cooke, Zach Martin, and Cris Welsh all went on to become Social Studies teachers. Noel Sudano works there as a guidance counselor. All four were in the school during the shooting and they all escaped without injury, as did their brothers and sisters. All of them decided to become educators because of the examples they saw in their own teachers on April 20th. They appreciated how their teachers reacted to the crisis and made them feel safe. All four were still working at Columbine in 2024.

Cris Welsh told 9News in Denver: *"I just couldn't imagine entering into another profession and having done so utilizing that profession anywhere else than Columbine High School."*

Mandy Cooke, who was a sophomore at Columbine during the shooting, had to read about the shooting her first day of college. At the time, becoming a teacher was the furthest thing from her mind. But eventually she concluded that Columbine was where she needed to be. She told *StoryCorps*:

> *"I weirdly feel proud that I walk into Columbine every day. I'm doing the job I always wanted to do, and I get to teach some of the best kids in the world."*

Educators at Columbine have a unique position among their peers. 25 years after the shooting, they still must field questions from people about the event. Whenever a mass shooting makes the news, calls come pouring in. From media to private citizens, everyone wants to know their thoughts and advice. Many of the staff feel strange about being the go-to as they don't feel they have any great insights into the crime or its outcome, yet they roll with it and try their best to assist information seekers. If they can bring any sort of positive out of what happened that day, they will.

APRIL 20, 2024

April 20, 2024. 25 years to the day after the shooting at Columbine.

It was still snowing that morning when Sean and I headed out, but it had shifted to a light, fluffy fall that painted everything in pure white. Again, I was reminded of 1999, and the blizzard that blanketed the memorials in Robert F. Clement Park that well-wishers had left. As we pulled up to the school, it looked just as it had in the photos taken over the week following the shooting.

In the parking lot a security guard questioned us, checked our credentials, then allowed us to park. It was a necessary precaution: In the past they've had people try to sneak on campus. One reporter went so far as to dress up like a student, backpack and all, attempting to gain access to the school. Once, a whole charter bus showed up and offloaded a group of people who were there on a "Gore Tour" that traveled to various infamous locations in the United States. They arrived while school was in session, expecting to be allowed to wander around wherever they pleased because they'd paid the company for a tour. The company didn't have permission to be there, so the group had to leave. While I was there, there were three separate incidents I know of where an individual tried to come onto the school grounds. Additionally, there were at least two groups of reporters stationed across the street taking pictures of people and the school.

Driving around the senior lot to the side of Columbine, I saw the entrance to the cafeteria for the first time in person. I couldn't help looking to the spot where Daniel Rohrbough died. It was a plain stretch of sidewalk, no different than the rest. It wasn't the original sidewalk: That slab of concrete was given to his family, which they turned into the base of a swing in their backyard. A permanent memorial to his life and loss. Looking up the hill, the distance between the stairs and the common area in front of the school was smaller than I thought. Photos make the school seem a lot bigger than it is.

In addition to reporters and trespassers, Columbine was receiving a decent amount of traffic that was supposed to be there as the 8th Annual Day of Service was just getting started. A check-in table was set up inside the vestibule of the main entrance of the school. In the office to the right, Dunkin Donuts and t-shirts awaited those who had signed up to come tie blankets and perform other community service projects.

Sean and I were met in the entryway by our SRO connection, Eric Ebling. He had a long history with Columbine starting when he was a teen who attended the 1999 prom with a girl who was a student at the school. He took us on a tour, and we talked about the history of the shooting, which my friend Sean was largely unfamiliar with. We hadn't spoken much about the actual shooting the night before at the house party. That event was about healing and moving forward. But before the memorial service, it was the right time to talk about the past. Ebling and I gave him the speedrun version of what happened, calling out specific events as we passed significant areas of the building.

It was the first time I set foot in the school, though I was familiar enough from my extensive research that I knew the layout by heart. As I mentioned before, I didn't go sooner because the school is not a tourist destination. It's not a museum or a time capsule. It's a school that is still running. The people who work and learn there deserve privacy and the right to carry on in a manner as normal as they can. Having been there, I can honestly say that there is very little for the average person to see. Even if you know exactly where everything happened, there are no lingering traces from the tragedy. The library is gone. The areas where people died are clean, free of damage. There are only painted murals of flowers and stained-glass window hangings that signify where Rachel Scott and Coach William "Dave" Sanders died.

Many things have changed since the shootings, in the world and at Columbine specifically. During my visit I noticed changes instituted at the school over the years. Most notably, the west entrance where Rachel Scott was killed had been extended to connect the HOPE Memorial Library to the school hallway. When it was constructed, the library was originally a stand-alone building atop the hill outside the school. With the added enclosed connection, students no longer had to go outside to access the library.

The extended entrance looked the same as the old one, but further out. SRO Ebling pointed out a ripple in the tiled floor and noted that was where the old entrance had been. He also pointed out the location where Rachel died. Then he let us out through the west doors for a look at the sports fields. He had to unlock the doors first. A sign posted in the window announced that no students were allowed to use the exit. It was an emergency exit only, kept locked when not actively in use.

The cafeteria downstairs changed significantly. The tables used to have detached chairs. The current tables have stools that are connected to the table base. During the shooting, students stampeding from the room tripped over and threw chairs, causing avoidable injuries. Another change in the cafeteria: They no longer serve Chinese or Japanese food. Teriyaki chicken was on the menu the day of the shooting, and many associated the smell with the tragic event.

I noticed throughout our tour how much smaller the campus seemed compared to photos. Even looking at the pictures I took while I was there, the place looks bigger than it feels when you're inside it. Despite being two stories and fully outfitted with a gym and auditorium, it doesn't take much time to get around the campus. With an average student count of around 1,800, there isn't a need for more space. The parking lots, too, seemed a lot smaller in person than they do when you're looking at a map of the property or aerial photos.

The library was another place where changes were made. They put in a floor-to-ceiling memorial stone that features the names of the students and faculty member who were killed. Next to it, a quilt made of T-shirts from past years was hung. Ebling pointed out a narrow window across the hall from the stone of names that was put in with the intention to allow passersby to see the memorial display. However, too many trespassers on the property over the years had forced them to shut out the public and keep the area under tight watch. After hearing the radio broadcasts that day, I understand the need for caution.

While curiosity about the school is understandable, there really is no need to come to the place. There have been so many photos taken inside and out that a personal trip there isn't necessary and is entirely unwelcome if you haven't been invited there. If you call ahead and make plans with campus security, you might be permitted to visit the viewing window with an escort. Those who come onto school property without permission will be cited for trespassing.

While the memorial in the library is a nice touch, it isn't worth getting arrested over. Nothing at Columbine is. It is just a school. It doesn't feel haunted. There are no tell-tale bullet holes, or anything to be seen that is related to the tragedy. If you didn't know where the old library was, you would never recognize the area where the entrance used to be. Even standing right next to the windows that looked out over the atrium, I was hard-pressed to imagine what the doorway would have looked like back in the day. And I've seen photos of it.

COLUMBINE NOW

Another subtle change: The auditorium downstairs now bears a plaque that designates it the Andres Auditorium, after teachers Leland and Lee Andres, who both were instrumental in protecting students that day. To anyone who hasn't studied their Columbine history, one would never know why it's named that.

As new schools are built in Colorado and abroad, it is done with an eye to security, and the safety of those who will be there. Though a school will have multiple exits, there is usually only one or two ways to enter the campus, and those entrances are monitored by security. In 2018, the Federal School Safety Commission examined how statutes and regulations have changed. Among them are the subjects of character development and culture of connectedness, cyberbullying, mental health and counseling, anonymous reporting, security, active shooter preparedness, and training of school personnel.

Something else that has changed at Columbine and many other schools throughout the United States is that in addition to fire drills, the school now has lockdown drills and secure perimeter drills. The National Center for Education Statistics says that 96% of schools in the United States now has a written plan for active shooter situations. Regardless of the drill, faculty at Columbine High are careful to announce in advance any drill they intend to have so those who might be triggered can plan to avoid the school that day. The drills are vetted as well. Drills that are too realistic could have the risk of causing emotional and psychological harm in participants. In that same vein of logic, the school no longer shows war movies in class.

Jeff Pierson, the executive director of Safety and Security at Jefferson County Public Schools, oversees 160 security personnel for the district, some of whom are armed. Pierson is a highly decorated police officer with FEMA and RAID certification. Responsible for the SROs in Denver's schools, he places priority on training new staff in how to manage incidents and to take their responsibilities seriously. All new school principals are trained at the Frank DeAngelis Community Safety Center where they are given scenarios to work through. They focus on emergency prevention as well as response. Prevention is preferable to reaction. JeffCo also has an emergency management team, campus supervisors, and threat assessment teams. There was no shortage of security during my visit to Columbine on April 20th, 2024.

After the tour, SRO Ebling allowed us to explore on our own until it was time for the reading of the names of the victims in the library. While we were wandering, we saw people of all ages engaging throughout the school, smiling and working together. There was positive energy everywhere.

At 11:00 a.m. Sean and I went to the library where we met and spoke with Principal Scott Christy. Then we met former principal Frank DeAngelis. Mr. De was calling the families of the victims, a ritual he did every year at that time. He spared us some of his time to learn who we were and to speak with us about his experiences and how he was doing. Even though it's been a quarter of a century, I could see the pain in his eyes when he talked about certain aspects of the tragic event. But he spoke positively of the changes that have come since then, changes to official protocols on how to handle such events and changes in the way society deals with mental instability, drug use in teens, and potential threats. We hugged and promised to stay in contact.

The 25th year brought only a small number of people to the school for the memorial. These included Dawn Anna, mother of victim Lauren Townsend; Darrell Scott, father of victim Rachel Scott; Craig Scott, Rachel's brother; a handful of faculty members and students who had been at the school during the shooting; the executive director of JeffCo's administrators' association; the current principal (as of 2024) Scott Christy, and former principal Frank DeAngelis. Known as Mr. De to friends and students, he retired as principal in 2014 after 18 years. Still, every year, he heads to Columbine's library to recite the names of the thirteen who were killed on April 20th.

At 11:15, the reading of the names began. He doesn't need to read the teleprompter; they are etched indelibly into his soul as he says those names every morning. 25 years after the shooting, his voice still hitches with emotion as he works his way through that list. In years past, that reading has been a somber exercise and when it ended, the shadow of the tragedy still loomed. This year, it was different.

The weather has always been odd during these emotional times. The Columbine area enjoyed pleasant Spring weather the week before the tragedy. When the shooters' bodies were removed from the school on the 21st, a blizzard started. At the Columbine Memorial groundbreaking on June 16, 2006, it was pouring rain. It came time to start the ceremony. Dawn Anna, who was at the groundbreaking, said to those gathered: *"They're here. Can you feel them? Our angels."* Then she gave her dedication speech. At poignant times when she was speaking, thunder pealed. It was as though the heavens were agreeing with and amplifying her powerful message. At the end, the rain stopped. The clouds parted and a beautiful rainbow appeared behind Rebel Hill.

It had been snowing since the night before. As Mr. De gave his speech of encouragement in which spoke of the future and moving forward, we could see sunlight breaking through the clouds outside. Glimpses of blue sky. He called it out as he wrapped up with a new message for the days to come: Hope.

The mindset among the attendees of the 25th year memorial was the same as the weather: There had been dark, cold days, but it was time to embrace and create brighter times. Everyone I spoke with that day said the same thing. I even overheard strangers at Clement Park echo the sentiment. It was finally time to step out of the shadows of the tragedy and focus on making the future better. SRO Ebling said it best when he declined to come listen to the reading of the names in the library.

"I've been to it before. Several times now. I don't need to hear it again. I'm needed on the campus."

That is the focus of April 20th to those who survived it: To grow and heal. This was perfectly illustrated by something I saw as I left the school following the ceremony. There was a planter outside the main entrance covered by a white blanket of fresh fallen snow. Poking up through the snow were sturdy, brightly colored tulips that were just beginning to open their blooms. The flowers had survived the freezing temperatures and the harsh weather and stood strong.

Ready for the sun that was coming.

MOVING FORWARD

The feeling at Columbine High School during the 25th anniversary reflected a need to remember while moving forward into productive outlets. Everywhere I looked there were people hugging and supporting one another. There were kids doing community projects, smiling and working well together. Though there were tears in the library around the time of the shooting, overall, the energy at the school was positive and uplifting. It felt like a window had opened and a fresh, healing breeze was flowing through.

When we finished saying our goodbyes to those we'd met at Columbine High, Sean and I went over to the Columbine Memorial at Clement Park. Completed in September 2007, the memorial consists of a Ring of Remembrance in the center that features placards for the victims that bear their names and a brief inscription about who they were. You can view the stone placards at https://www.columbinememorial.org/ring-of-remembrance/.

A Wall of Healing forms a semicircle on one side of the Ring, the side closest to Columbine. There is a water feature there, but it was turned off when I visited, possibly because of the cold. The memorial needed some maintenance. Some of the words on the placards were worn down and hard to read. There were a few other minor defects that could stand to be addressed, showing the need for financial support. The memorial costs roughly $10,000 to $15,000 per year to maintain. In 2024, the Columbine Memorial Foundation asked the community for even greater financial assistance to restore and upgrade the site. In addition to re-lettering the placards, the memorial needs a lighting upgrade. The Foundation estimated the lighting alone would cost roughly $50,000. (You can contribute to the cause here: https://www.columbinememorial.org/donate/.)

Despite the snow there were several visitors, including a woman who had crafted and posted 13 small crosses along the path leading to the memorial garden. As I passed, I overheard her telling some onlookers that when she gave birth to her daughter, she had given her the middle name "Cassie" after one of the victims. In one of the flower beds beyond her display, someone had created 13 little snowmen which sat on the brick pavers that shaped the planter. There were fresh flowers on every name placard in the center of the memorial. Everywhere I went in the memorial grounds, I caught snatches of conversation. Most of it revolved around hope for the future rather than despair for the past. After 25 years, the Columbine community was ready to look for blue skies among the clouds.

As I wandered about feeling the somber yet peaceful vibe the memorial gave off, I noticed in one of the planters under a clump of snow was another patch of bright tulips. Like the ones I saw at the school, these sturdy flowers were poking their colorful heads up in defiance of the icy blanket that tried to smother them. Green and pink and yellow against a white field. Another glimpse of hope and renewal.

PATH TO HEALING

As time has passed, many people who were directly affected by the Columbine shooting have turned from analyzing what happened and why to the healing path of making some good come from the experience. It's an excellent approach to a situation beyond your control. We can't choose the tragic turns life can sometimes throw at us, but we can choose how to deal with them. Using our experiences to do something that benefits others can be very rewarding.

I lost my parents and my spouse of 25 years over the span of 6 years. I discovered that when I was busy volunteering at children's hospitals, I didn't have time to get lost in my grief. It wasn't denial: I could take the stages of grief in doses and then busy myself again with something I had to pay attention to. I could give myself permission to be happy while I helped sick

MOVING FORWARD

kids take their minds off being stuck at the hospital. Put my mind on positive things rather than stewing on the negative, for their sake if nothing else. The same seems to be true of many of the survivors of the Columbine shooting. By helping others, they are helping themselves.

Coni Sanders, the daughter of slain victim Coach Dave Sanders, has taken that route. She works as a forensic therapist dealing with violent offenders. She wants to better understand their behavior to help prevent other people from becoming victims of violent crime like her father. She feels it is time to make forward strides. She told *TIME*:

"I think a lot of us are looking at it and saying, OK, we're done talking about that day. We're done talking about where we were, how we found out. Now let's talk about what we can do together, what we can do about it."

Rachel Scott's family took up an ongoing crusade in her name, Rachel's Challenge, to celebrate her life and help them to forgive, and move on. Other families have set up scholarships in honor of their loved ones.

Patrick Ireland, the "boy in the window" prefers to take a different approach. Though he has spoken with the media over the years about his experience, he prefers to forget the shooters' names and move on with his life. He learned through therapy and rehab how to put aside his anger and dismiss the individuals who very nearly killed him. Instead, he focuses on doing everything he can to improve his situation in life. In 2019 he told 9News:

"The key to forgiveness is to stop focusing on what people have done to us, and to focus on the healing, the blessing of what people have done for us."

In April 2000, the Harrises and Klebolds wrote public letters of apology to the victims of the shooting, released through their attorneys.

The Harrises' letter:

A COLUMBINE BOOK – WE ARE ALL COLUMBINE

We continue to be profoundly saddened by the suffering of so many that has resulted from the acts of our son. We loved our son dearly and search our souls daily for some glimmer of a reason why he would have done such a horrible thing. What he did was unforgivable and beyond our capacity to understand. The passage of time has yet to lessen the pain.

We are thankful to those who have kept us in their thoughts and prayers."

– Wayne and Kathy Harris

And the Klebolds:

Nearly a year has passed since tragedy changed the Columbine community forever. A day that began innocently ended catastrophically. The healing process has moved slowly as we all attempt to cope, not only with our own despair, but also with the distractions and intrusions that result from world attention.

There are no words to convey how sorry we are for the pain that has been brought upon the community as a result of our son's actions. The pain of others compounds our own as we struggle to live a life without the son we cherished. In the reality of the Columbine tragedy and its aftermath, we look with the rest of the world to understand how such a thing could happen.

We are convinced that the only way to truly honor all of the victims of this and other related tragedies is to move clearly and methodically toward an understanding of why they occur, so that we may try to prevent this kind of madness from ever happening again. It is our intention to work for this end, believing that answers are probably within reach, but that they will not be simple. We envision a time when circumstances will allow us to join with those who share our desire to understand. In the meantime, we again express our profound condolences to those whose lives have been so tragically altered. We look forward to a day when all of our pain is replaced by peace and acceptance.

MOVING FORWARD

Finally, we wish to thank those who have sent their kind thoughts, prayers and expressions of support to our family. We are constantly surprised and heartened by the gestures of understanding and compassion that have been extended to us. The support has been both humbling and inspiring, and we are truly indebted to those who have offered it.

– the Klebold family

Since that time, Sue Klebold became a public speaker and authored books about her experience as the mother of an infamous shooter. Initially, her efforts were largely met with criticism from the public, but over time her contributions have gained interest and respect. Several of the Columbine families have openly stated they no longer harbor anger or ill-will toward the Klebolds or the Harrises. Coni Sanders has even forged a friendship with Sue Klebold. She says of the friendship:

"A lot of people will reference forgiveness in relation to my friendship with Sue Klebold. I have nothing to forgive her for. She didn't do this."

Sanders, whose father was killed by Dylan, was initially frustrated and angry at the shooters' parents. After she had kids of her own, her opinion changed. When she met with Klebold, that opinion solidified. Going into her first meeting with the mother of her father's killer, she wanted Klebold to be awful. A terrible parent would justify a terrible child who could commit mass murder. But Sanders was taken by surprise at how compassionate and comforting Klebold was. At the end of that first meeting they hugged. It was the start of a friendship that would continue over the years. They often talk about ways to create something powerful and impactful together. Sanders told CBN:

"If anybody's pain is greater than my own, in my eyes, it's hers."

Some of the Columbine families including that of John Tomlin expressed early on that they harbored no ill will toward the parents. Beth Nimmo, mother of slain victim Rachel Scott, empathized with the plight the Klebolds and Harris faced. Her family, she said, had the support of the community while they were stigmatized and hated. She told the *Denver Post* in April 2000: *"As a mother, they're not different from me. They loved those boys."*

Maya Angelou, a famous poet, said: *"Forgiveness is a gift you give yourself."*

After 25 years, even Isaiah Shoels' father Michael who was adamant in his refusal to forgive the killers or their families said it's time. He chooses now to forgive, though he will never forget. And as difficult as it is for him to return to Colorado, every year he goes back to visit his son's grave. When the Shoels picked the location where Isaiah would be buried, they selected a plot that had a small tree beside it. Now, when his family returns, they see a strong, fully grown tree towering over Isaiah's gravestone. Michael, who like many of the Columbine families, harbors frustration over how little has changed culturally and politically over the years.

"To me, that tree represents growth. And the children are our future. The children are the roots of our nation. If we keep on letting them get killed and we keep on letting them die so early… what're we going to do?"

Craig Scott, like many of the survivors, had a lot of hate in him he had to learn to let go of after the gunmen killed his friends and sister. Holding onto it led him to become aggressive. It started to take a toll on his personality, making him more hostile. More like the people he hated so much. One day after a fight with his brother, he realized that without intending to he was becoming like the people who had wronged him. It was a conscious decision on his part to let go of that hate and anger, and to focus on helping others. By helping them, he helped himself to see the good in life again.

Scott has since come to a point where he can let go of that anger. Things changed when he was invited to take his sister's place on a mission to Africa with a church youth group. While ministering to people in refugee camps there, Scott encountered people who had suffered more losses than he had. Being with them taught him he could heal through forgiveness. Scott became a public speaker at the age of 18 and has spoken to millions of people over the years. He now owns his own film production company and works with the outreach charity his father created: Rachel's Challenge. He emphasizes the importance of staying focused on the good life has to offer. By 2019, over twelve million people had heard Rachel's life story.

Focusing on the negative is what he feels fed into why the shooting happened to begin with. Harris focused on his hatred of others while Klebold focused on his hatred of himself. He told the *Christian Post* that when someone asked him how a school shooter could do what they did, his response was:

"Imagine that you just started seeing the worst in everybody and everything, disconnecting yourself from other people, and then choosing very negative, hateful influences through media... Now, can you see how it could happen?"

Scott believes forgiveness is a major step on the path to healing; that holding onto negative emotions for years just makes a person a prisoner of unforgiveness. Author Lewis B. Smedes said: *"To forgive is to set a prisoner free and discover that the prisoner was you."*

CHANGE FOR THE FUTURE

Change is seldom easy, but often necessary. This is very much the case with the circumstances surrounding Columbine. Klebold and Harris didn't kick start a revolution, but they did draw attention to the fact that the education system in the US has desperately needed change for decades, as has our stance on firearms. The question is: How to bring about those changes?

Twenty-five years after the tragic shooting, we are still no closer to an answer. In schools, "zero tolerance" policies haven't fixed things and, in most cases, has only made school a more hostile and prison-like environment. The kind of change we need isn't going to be found in stricter dress codes and suspension. It's something that needs to be affected at a root level, starting as early as kindergarten.

The basic points that need the most adjusting in education are:

- Teacher retention
- Classroom and student body size
- Emphasis on Arts and Academics beyond Math, Science, and English
- Balance between the Athletics and Academics
- Parental engagement
- Better social connections within school
- Effective anti-violence programs

Back in the pioneer days, school was a one-room class that served the children of a small community. There were likely to be no more than a dozen kids taught by a school marm or master who taught to their age and capability. Students were given individual attention by someone who stood in as both an educator and caregiver. Teachers were in regular contact with parents. They knew the children's families and were acquainted with what their home life was like. Even in that close-knit environment classism and bullying took place, but it was easier to catch and curtail.

Most public schools and many private ones in the USA are overcrowded. The national average in the US of students to teachers was roughly 16:1 in 2018 according to the National Center for Education Statistics (NCES), the statistical center within the U.S. Department of Education's Institute of Education Sciences (IES). In 2023, the Los Angeles Unified School District reported that their ratio sat at close to 35:1. In the 2022-2023 school year, Jefferson County School District of Colorado had just 330 guidance counselors and 67 psychologists for over

MOVING FORWARD

77,000 students. That's 223 kids per guidance counselor and 1,149 kids for each psychologist.

Ideally, smaller classrooms and more individualized attention would be the way to go. But the reality is that teachers are underpaid and hard to find. According to USA Today in 2023, 86% of schools struggled to find educators. 9 out of 10 public schools found it difficult to fill their teaching positions. A 2022 report by the US Department of Education said that 41 states are experiencing shortages of teachers. The pool of educators is diminishing by the year and there aren't enough people entering the field to replace them. Burn-out, low pay, feeling undervalued, and dysfunctional workplaces are the biggest barriers to retaining teaching staff.

With schools cutting budgets for the Arts and other "non-core" classes, teachers are forced to provide resources for themselves. This is compounded by the imbalance between academic classes and athletics. Coaches are more greatly prized at many schools than other teachers, with some schools paying coaches twice as much as their highest paid English teacher. In many schools, coaches take roles as academic teachers as well. Columbine has a sports coach who is also the high school wood shop teacher. My own high school's football coach was my Social Studies teacher. According to the Sport Journal, more than 40% of full-time secondary educators have some sort of coaching responsibility. And while a good teacher can make a good coach and vice versa, conflicts of interest can arise. Parents, fans, players, boosters, the community, and school administrators can pressure the individual to favor their coaching duties over academics. Coaching can take priority if time, energy, or resources are short.

To a greater degree this is what has been happening in the schools: When the budget and hiring pool are strained, athletics take precedence. The public school district in my area has systematically pared down the Art program until there is exactly one (1) Art teacher for all of the schools. That's one teacher for 36,000 students. There are two (2) orchestra teachers for the district. All three of these teachers have to float from school to school, driving long hours for diminishing pay in a time when the cost of living is on the rise.

An issue that's even trickier to solve is the one of parental engagement. Modern society is rife with broken homes, parents who work more than one job, parents and guardians who are actively using drugs, and a general lack of secure bonds between parents and children. Many adults treat school like child storage: They drop the kid off and the child is someone else's responsibility, someone else's problem, for eight hours. With their personal schedules packed and precariously balanced between earning money and scavenging a personal life they've been told by society they deserve many adults don't want to engage with the school system any more than they absolutely must.

Over the years, parental involvement with schools has declined as more adults choose to interact with the school system through Internet portals. In the 2017-2018 school year, the NCES reported that 45% of parents of high school students filled out a parent-school cooperation contract while less than 1% were involved in anything outside of "special events" such as concerts (29%) and budget matters (2%). In all categories except budget there was a significant drop in parental involvement between middle and secondary education.

The environment at school is important as well, and something that has seen significant change over the years. Interestingly, it was COVID rather than Columbine that ushered in the most change where it comes to supporting the emotional and social support of students, with 90% of schools in the US reporting to the NCES they had increased this support following the pandemic. The two factors that limited schools in their ability to reduce/prevent crime and bullying came down to inadequate placements or programs for disruptive students and inadequate funding. Despite this, secondary schools reported a 1% drop in drug distribution and in hate crimes in the 2021-22 school year compared with that of the 2017-18 school year. Data gathered by the NCES indicates that reports of at least one incident of bullying per week are more prevalent in middle school (28%) than secondary school (15%).

In 2021-22, 92% of US schools said they had a plan in place to deal with a pandemic and bomb threats, and 96% had plans to deal with active shooters and natural disasters. What's more, 72% of charter schools reported having restorative practices in 2019-20. 59% of public schools did, which is lower than the charter schools, but was still up from 42% in the 2018-19 school year.

Restorative practices (also known as restorative justice) focus on strengthening the bonds and relationships between individuals, youth and adult, in school communities. Schools have also taken on more programs over the years that deal with safe reporting. Columbine High now has a "tip box" in the main hall and a couple of different mediation processes that facilitate problem resolution for students, including Safe2Tell.

YOUR ROLE

Something I've long believed is that happiness is a choice. I think I first saw the notion printed on a motivational poster or bumper sticker. "Choose Happy" it said. Others have echoed this sentiment throughout time. Aeschylus said: *"Happiness is a choice that requires effort sometimes."* Ironically, this Greek playwright is considered the father of tragedy thanks to his plays.

Sadhguru Darnash, a spiritual leader and head of the Isha Foundation, said we should start the day with a smile. Not a smile at anyone but because we are alive. One more day of life is one more day of possibilities and hope. It's a great philosophy because no matter what happens throughout the day, you've already started off looking for good. You've opened your mind to positivity and accomplished something.

A close friend of mine likes to say about smiles: *"If you see someone without a smile, give them one of your own. It's free and you never know... you might just get one back."*

What we look for in life, we find. If you are constantly looking for negative messages... well. They're super easy to find. Just look at the news. Negative messages everywhere. Choosing to surround yourself with those messages reinforces that dark narrative. Conversely, if you actively seek out videos on YouTube that feature people helping each other, you will find it. Seek positivity and positivity will surround you.

A lot of times, the focus of situations such as the Columbine shooting is on the perpetrators, their mentality, and the damage they caused to life and the fabric of the community they terrorized. It's human instinct to want to understand aberrant behavior if for no other reason than to recognize and avoid it when we encounter it. It's not bad to want to know more. It's not wrong to insist on getting the truth. But when that quest becomes a rabbit hole that leads you to dark places, it's time to switch tactics. Holding onto hate for or fascination with the victimizers can quickly become unhealthy for one's mind and lifestyle.

Because the people and the situation surrounding the Columbine shooting is so relatable, there is a real risk that researchers face when tunneling into the subject. There are many out there who idealize events such as this one without truly researching the full effects and situation. But one can be interested in subjects such as the Columbine shooting without idealizing or becoming fixated on them in an unhealthy manner. It's all about balance and being open to accepting painful truths.

The best way to handle the bad stuff in life is to get what you need from it and then let it go. There's a time for grief. A time for anger. There's a time to defend your position and there's a time to take what you've learned and try to turn it into something positive for the future. Nothing in life can stay put in one place for too long. Rooting down is something best left to plants. Animals and humans that stay still too long begin to atrophy and decay. We must keep pushing forward. We need to forge a path that will make it easier for those who follow behind us to take over when we're gone.

There are many ways you can make a difference—in your life, in your community, and in the world. In life, we each are tasked with deciding how to spend our time. There is nothing wrong in finding contentment where you're at, if you're not hurting yourself or anyone else. But if you really want to make a lasting difference, the best way to do it is to get involved. Helping charities, becoming an activist for good causes, running for public office, or even just strengthening bonds with your family can make a difference. The more you do, the bigger an impact you will have. If you're going to be remembered for something, being remembered for making a positive difference is easy to achieve. It starts with deciding to be the change you want to see in the world.

CONCLUSION

So where do we go from here? In some ways, things have changed for the better while in other ways, things are far worse. The political landscape of 2024 feels reminiscent of the 1980s. The United States is in a state of culture war with itself. People tune out of the real world and immerse themselves in cellphones and laptop computers, shutting out the people around them with noise-canceling headphones that isolate them and erode the sense of community. Worldwide there are troubles that seem almost insurmountable with tragedies mounting by the day.

It's a time when we need hope more than ever.

FINAL THOUGHTS

After 25 years of writing about Columbine, my visit to the school has brought a sense of closure to the project. The website will remain up for researchers worldwide to access. I still believe there needs to be a free, unbiased source for people to get information from, especially now that the event truly is history. In tandem with the publication of this book and its companion book about the event itself (*A Columbine Book : Who. What. Where. When. Why?*) I feel the story is told to the best of my ability with the information I have. I will always welcome discussion about it, particularly with those who had to experience the event firsthand. But it's time for my focus to shift to other things and new ways to help people.

One way I'm doing that is by keeping the Day of Service rolling in my own community. I encourage you to do the same where you live. There's a place on their website (https://www.columbineserves.org) where you can let the united Columbine family know what project(s) you're doing to connect

CONCLUSION

you with the group effort. Charity's a funny thing: The more you do, the more you get inspired to do.

The future may be uncertain, but if we all do our best to make positive change and to approach the world with a loving attitude – love for our environment, our community, and ourselves – we can make it a less hostile and lonely world. Change comes from all sizes of steps. Like the steady drip of water from a cave ceiling growing a stalagmite, something big can come from even the smallest persistent action.

+

Sunday, April 21, 2024. It was time for me to leave Colorado. By then, the temperature in Denver was edging up toward the 70s again. The bad weather had cleared, and the clouds were gone. It was nothing but blue skies and pleasant weather the whole way home.

REFERENCES & RESOURCES

Columbine High School

Columbine High School faculty

Jefferson County Sheriff's Department

JeffCo Administrators Association

Frank DeAngelis

They Call Me Mr. De by Frank DeAngelis

A Columbine Site – http://www.aColumbineSite.com

International Association of Chiefs of Police

   Active shooter protocol – https://www.theiacp.org/sites/default/files/2021-07/ActiveShooter2018-UpdatedFormat%2007.16.2021_0.pdf

Rachel's Challenge - https://rachelschallenge.org/

Columbine Memorial – 7306 W. Bowles Avenue, Littleton, CO. 80123

   Donate: Columbine Memorial Foundation, Inc. P.O. Box 621636, Littleton, CO. 80162-1636

Frank DeAngelis Columbine High School Academic Foundation

The Rebels Project https://www.therebelsproject.org

Sean Reavie

Eric Ebling

John DeStefano

Comprehending Columbine by Ralph W. Larkin, Ph.D.

Mauser family

Dawn Anna

Rohrbough and Petrone families

Krista Hanley

Patrick Ireland

Kacey Ruegsegger Johnson

Brian Anderson

Craig Scott

Linda and Coni Sanders

Tomlin family

CNN – https://www.cnn.com/

Denver Post Online – http://www.denverpost.com

Rocky Mountain News – http://rockymountainnews.com/

Westword – https://www.westword.com/

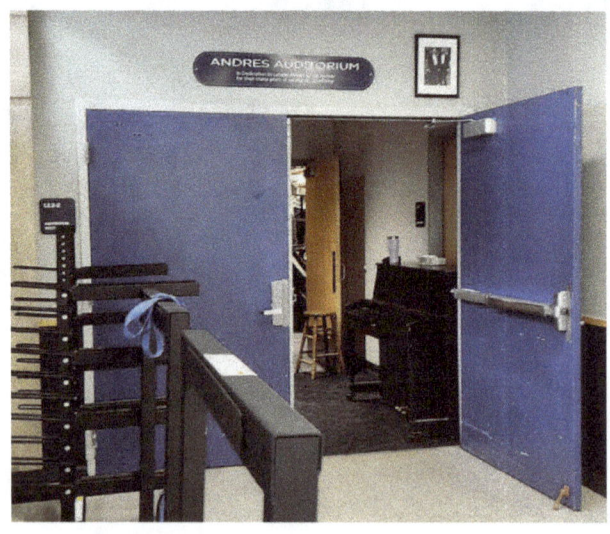

A COLUMBINE BOOK – WE ARE ALL COLUMBINE

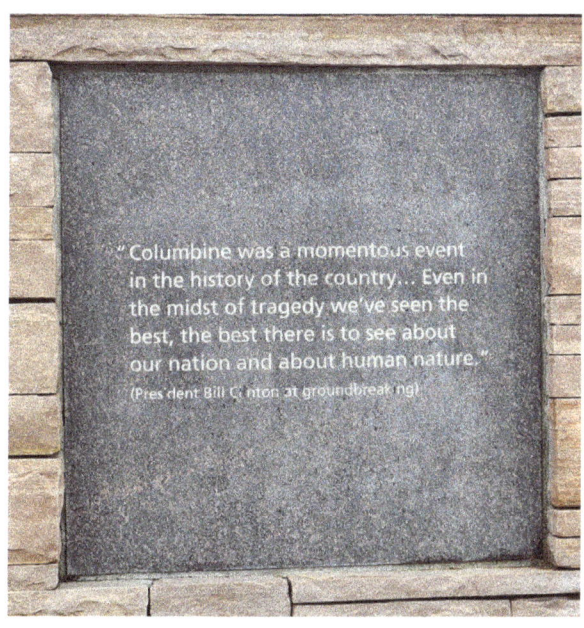

ABOUT THE AUTHOR

I wrote and have been maintaining the Internet's oldest site about Columbine, http://www.aColumbineSite.com, since April 21, 1999. The site sees over 1,000,000 visitors annually and is free to use by anyone across the globe.

    In addition to being credited in multiple best-selling books about Columbine, my writing has been referenced by families of the victims and by law enforcement for official disaster-readiness plans in the USA, Australia, Malaysia, and other locations. I've assisted journalists, teachers, students, authors, playwrights, and film directors with their Columbine projects. I've also appeared in short educational films and documentaries about the subject.

    I hold an associate's degree with an emphasis on Film and Forensic Science. I'm a member of the Clara Barton Society and am an active member of charity groups that work with survivors of trauma and abuse. I've volunteered at police and school events for over 20 years, with the last nine spent helping the Crimes Against Children division of my local police department. In 2009, the Fort Wayne police department presented me with a certificate of appreciation for assisting them in developing their crisis training program. In 2024, I was honored to receive the Columbine High School Challenge Coin from the Denver Police.

If you found this book helpful, please leave a 5-star review on Amazon. It helps others find it.

https://amzn.to/3AlN82u

A NOTE ABOUT CONTACT WITH THE SURVIVORS:

I have been in contact with some of the people who lived through this tragic event, but only those who have been receptive to my initial inquiries. I have not tried to dig up contact information for anyone who has not made it publicly available. I don't want to make anyone uncomfortable or dredge up pain they wish to leave behind. I do not share contact information I do have, so please don't request it.

If you are someone who experienced this tragedy first-hand and want to share your story with me or request corrections, you can reach me at aColumbineSite@gmail.com.

www.ingramcontent.com/pod-product-compliance
Lightning Source LLC
Chambersburg PA
CBHW070453100426
42743CB00010B/1601